BIG FISH

BIG FISH

Secrets to Hooking and Landing the Best Clients in Any Industry

JAMES CRAIG COLLYER

ISBN-13: 9781530617265
ISBN-10: 153061726X
Library of Congress Control Number: 2017903311
CreateSpace Independent Publishing Platform
North Charleston, South Carolina

Cover and interior illustrations by Eric Endy.

Photographs by Michelle Guthrie

For
Michelle

ACKNOWLEDGMENTS

This book would not have been possible without the support and encouragement of many people.

First, I would like to thank all the business owners and salespeople who unselfishly shared their best sales tips with me. Your guidance and support is appreciated. Second, I would like to thank my many clients. You have inspired me to keep teaching this sales method, because I've seen the incredible results you have achieved in a short period of time. Thank you for proving time and again that relationship selling is the core to every business success. Next, I would like to thank all of my many mentors for showing me the way. I cherish all the times we spent together. The lessons won't be forgotten.

Lastly, a special thanks goes to Michelle Guthrie, whose contributions to this work made it possible. My gratitude and admiration are beyond words. Thank you. I couldn't have done it without you.

ABOUT THE AUTHOR

Jim Collyer is a sales executive, trainer, and best-selling author living in Nevada. Collyer has received the Editors Choice award, the Pinnacle award, and the Moving America Forward award. Collyer has coauthored works with such notables as Sir Richard Branson, Harvey Mackay, and Brian Tracy.

Growing up in the small logging and mining towns of Idaho, Collyer began his long, successful career in business at the age of ten, mowing lawns and delivering newspapers. Even at that early age, Jim had a talent for recognizing opportunities, implementing strategies, and making money.

Collyer's career includes numerous business start-ups, wholesale and retail, business consulting and coaching, contracting, logging, mining, writing, and publishing.

Collyer has presented seminars and spoken in front of thousands of people. He writes articles, blogs, and books on success and business, all based on his own personal, hands-on experience. His writings are "specific" methods, techniques and approaches to doing business that anyone can use to start a business or expand his or her current sales.

For more information, visit http://jccollyer.com, and learn how Jim Collyer can help you and your team get trained, motivated, and on your way to meeting your sales goals.

TABLE OF CONTENTS

INTRODUCTION

This book isn't about fishing, though I draw a lot of analogies between fishing and business success. The fish I'm writing about here are of the two-legged type. This book is about how to attract and hold the very best clients—*The Big Fish*—in any industry.

Big clients are hard to land. They don't want to be sold to, and that's why it's so difficult to do business with them.

Sure, there will be those occasional accidents in one's sales career when all of the stars line up and a big client will contact you requesting your service or products, but in the day-to-day reality of business, this probably isn't going to happen.

Why? In the first place, numbers. Really big clients comprise a very small percentage of the overall customer base. Big clients are hard to find, hard to approach, and extremely difficult to sell to.

Secondly, there's the clutter. Let's face it: there's a boatload of people out there trying to make a sale. On any given day the average person is subjected to no fewer than three thousand sales impressions. Most of these come from television, radio, print, and the Internet.

The Internet is the most cluttered of all media. There are more than four million websites on the net today. Less than 5 percent of them actually make a profit. How is a potential client going to find you in all of this clutter?

The Internet feeds on our desire for instant success, and there is no end to the number of instant-success programs available on the web. But step-by-step success programs aren't enough, because sales are based on principles more than systems.

More than that, the average sales professional will not spend the time or make the effort required in learning how to approach extremely large clients. Everyone wants a big sale, everyone dreams about it, but few will expend the energy necessary to make it happen.

To a large extent, salespeople have been hampered by all of the published information about making sales. While there have been some detailed and useful things written about the subject, what often get the most attention are the so-called "quick fix" books.

Sadly, there are no quick fixes—never were, never will be. We live in a society that seeks immediate gratification in all aspects of life. We don't want to work for anything. Everyone's looking for the shortcut to success, as if you could buy it. People want success on the cheap, but success can't be had at "bargain-basement" prices. Imagine if you could pay twenty dollars for a book and be guaranteed success. As far as I know, no such book exists. If it did, we'd all be skinny, rich, and living on a beach somewhere.

The only real difference between those who become enormously successful in sales and those who do not is dedication and an understanding of the buying process. Obviously, I can't give you the perseverance needed to succeed. You'll have to find that within yourself. What I can give you are the strategies and tactics that work—and have worked over the years—to attract the best and biggest clients.

What I won't give you is any quick fixes. It takes time and practice to reach a professional level in any endeavor, and sales is no different. You'll have to work at it.

This book is a means to help you understand how to approach the problem of attracting bigger clients than the ones you're currently working with, and just maybe move you into the realm of a sales superstar.

Strangely enough, someone just getting started in sales may have a better chance of utilizing this information than a sales veteran. Without preconceived notions and ingrained ideas on how things are done, the novice could easily be the one who succeeds.

If people believe they're doing something right, it's really hard to convince them otherwise. Once the brain believes it knows something, it tends to accept only information that backs up that belief, even if the information is false.

While you may think you know what you're doing, I can assure you there's nothing worse than doing the wrong things well. While experience is the best teacher, it doesn't necessarily have to be your own experience you learn from. You can and should learn from others.

If you're serious about improving your results, knowledge is the key. Just remember there's a difference between knowing and learning. For example, I went on Amazon a couple of weeks ago just to see how many swimming books were in print. Amazon lists more than two hundred books on swimming. If I read all of those books, I would know a lot about swimming. But until I jump into the water, I won't be able to learn how to swim.

Business works much the same way. You can attend all the seminars and read all the books on business, but until you put the information to use, it won't do you any good.

If you're teachable and have the determination to succeed, then read on. If not, don't waste your time on this book—it won't do you any good.

Chapter 1

THE STRUGGLE IS REAL

*D*oing business with the biggest and best clients is the dream of nearly every sales professional. These are the clients with pockets deep enough to spend five, six, or even seven figures with us annually. We often refer to such clients as "Big Fish" and having them as primary customers will give any business unparalleled stability.

To build and maintain sustainable business with these Big Fish, you'll have to learn how to work smarter, not harder. Time is your biggest enemy. You won't need to work longer hours, but you will need to focus your attention on the activities that yield the greatest results.

Unfortunately, most people feel trapped. They feel they are too busy eking out a living to devote the time and energy necessary to attract big clients. What most sales professionals don't understand is that in the process of learning the ways to attract the very biggest clients, the smaller clients come easier. As you gain a greater knowledge of what makes big clients tick, your confidence and success will grow in all aspects of the sales process. By simplifying the most daunting aspect of the process—attracting bigger clients—you will find that everything else falls into place.

If you're like most business professionals, the biggest challenge you face every day is generating enough sales to keep the business moving upward. When it comes to generating sales, most people get stumped. Maybe you've put your neck on the line and started a business. You've given your heart and soul to this business, but your best efforts to obtain more sales have yielded poor results or none whatsoever.

Maybe you're the business owner who is trying to take his or her business to the next level. If you could just generate a little more business, you'd be over the hump.

Or, maybe you're a sales professional whose commissions are stagnant or even spiraling downward. You blame the economy, interest rates, and the government. It's just bad luck, and it's getting worse. If only things would change...Of course, you're not to blame; it's the business climate's fault.

The economy isn't to blame. Businesses struggle when they can't sell sufficient quantities of their product at a high enough price to remain solvent. The truth is that we all need more and bigger clients, and we need them now.

Chances are your product or service isn't unique. Nowadays, you can't throw a rock without hitting someone who's doing similar work. You can bet someone's producing a similar or nearly identical product somewhere.

"Well, if no one is willing to take responsibility we'll blame the economy."

Our dreams of success often seem like unattainable goals that only other people can achieve. We want a better life and even try a couple of new strategies. When they don't work out, we give up, accept things as they are, and move on. We convince ourselves that we're not cut out for success. We turn our attention back to the things we can control and retreat back into our comfort zone.

It's tempting for all of us to stay in our comfort zone; however, comfort is boring. It's nothing more than an attachment to the past, and the past is not a place where we can grow, improve, and make the necessary changes we need to move our businesses forward. We tell ourselves we want change. But there's a problem with change: While everyone needs it, no one really wants the uncertainty it brings.

Successful people view change as an opportunity for growth. Change gets uncomfortable fast, and it stays uncomfortable for a long time. That's the way change works. Get used to it. The answer isn't becoming comfortable with life's challenges; it's found in accepting the discomfort.

Honestly, there really isn't a lot of unchartered water out there. All of the problems we face in business have been solved by someone somewhere. That's right—there are people out there who have conquered problems similar to the ones you're currently facing. It's time to quit waiting and to find those answers. Instead of giving up, we need to seek the advice of others who have become successful through sales.

That's the purpose of this book: to share the principles and skills routinely employed by the most successful sales professionals so that readers can understand the hows and whys and the strategies necessary to achieve their desired results. You'll learn the exact actions to take to advance yourself, your ideas, and your company. You'll see exactly what actions you need to take to gain market share and expand your business, regardless of economic conditions. I promise you that the practical and proven ideas in this book will get you better sales results than you ever imagined possible.

Your goal needs to be more than making a profit. The goal should be to do things right. Hefty profits are the result of doing things right.

I've created my list of the four principles of hooking and landing the best clients to help you stay focused on how to do things right. You'll need to let go of your attachment to profit and focus on these principles to achieve the success you desire.

FOUR PRINCIPLES FOR HOOKING AND LANDING CLIENTS

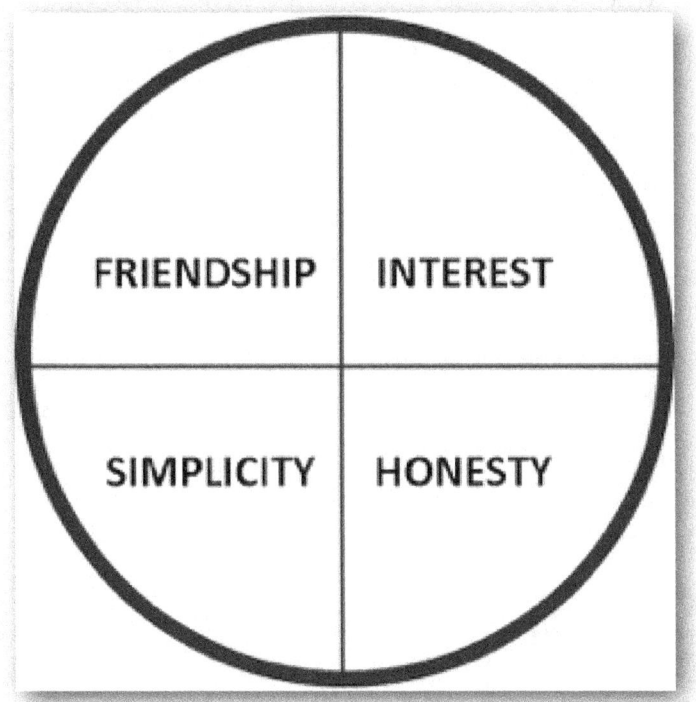

PRINCIPLE 1: FRIENDSHIP

In business, as in life, it's important to choose our friends wisely.

"In trying to please all, he had pleased none."—Aesop

Trying to gain everyone's business is useless. Your goal isn't to do business with everyone. Your goal is to do business with like-minded people who need your products and services.

How do we develop relationships with the best clients? How do we approach these clients? How do we determine which products are best suited to fill the needs of these clients? This is where working smarter and not harder comes into play.

PRINCIPLE 2: INTEREST

How do we get clients to pay attention to our products and services? How do we get them to care about doing business with us?

To do this we'll need to exceed their expectations and differentiate ourselves from the pack.

Most people think that gaining interest is a matter of generating curiosity. While generating curiosity is important, sustaining interest over a long period of time has more to do with caring than curiosity. No one will care about you and your business until you care about him or her first.

We'll need to shift the focus away from products and toward actively listening to our client talk about challenges.

PRINCIPLE 3: SIMPLICITY

Humans, as a species, have a tendency of overcomplicating even the simplest of ideas. We salespeople feel the need to impress our clients with the superior quality of our products or our knowledge of how things work. However, the opposite is true more often than not.

We have found that the more reasons we give a client to buy from us, the less likely the client will do so.

Simplicity requires that we find the core reason why the client should buy our product and that we convey that message to our prospect.

PRINCIPLE 4: HONESTY

Never exaggerate the capabilities or performance of your products or services. Your client will view you as a liar and lose trust in you instantly and forever.

Lies are like cockroaches—if your client sees one, he or she will know there are more around.

Honesty is a lot more than simply telling the truth. Telling the truth about our products and services is the easiest part of business. It's far more difficult to listen honestly, but it's a skill we must learn if we are going to be of any real help to our clients.

Honesty also requires us to treat our clients with the utmost dignity. We should never allow our client to do anything that isn't in his or her best interest, even at the cost of our losing a sale.

You probably already noticed that the Four Principles for Hooking and Landing Clients could be compacted into the acronym F.I.S.H. This was done intentionally to help you to understand and apply these principles in every situation. All of the principles are basic and seem to make common sense, so why isn't the world full of extremely successful sales professionals?

The problem is, these principles are so basic that they're easily overlooked. I'm not sure what it is about the basics that allow them to be ignored, but fewer than 5 percent of sales professionals apply these principles effectively. These principles are so important that I've devoted a chapter in this book to each of them.

There seems to be no end to the number of business "How-to" books available. Unfortunately, the authors of most of these books have limited or no experience in sales. They promise huge success but offer us little more than inspirational chit-chat. I believe spirit and enthusiasm are great if you're a cheerleader, but business is a little more complicated than that.

One expert tells us to be bold and another tells us to be humble. Some claim that marketing is the key to success, while others say to focus on product development. That's a lot of conflicting advice. While many of these authors make valid points, nearly all of them tend to overlook the necessity of the sale. Without a sale, nothing else happens. It doesn't matter how good your product or service is...if you can't sell it effectively, you will soon be out of business.

Sales truly are the lifeblood of any business. Given enough sales, any business is successful. When sales fall off, however, any business is at risk of failure. We need to sell as though our life depends on it, because it does.

If my experience as a sales trainer has taught me anything, it's this: the number-one obstacle preventing ambitious people from making more sales is *a misconception of the sales process and how the marketplace actually works*. Ambition without market knowledge is like gasoline without an engine. It burns wildly and gets you nowhere.

So much of what people have heard about the sales process is pure fantasy. Hollywood films and other media often present sales professionals as scam artists and swindlers; business owners and top corporate executives are portrayed as evil nincompoops.

We've all seen those movies in which business succeeds at the expense of working-class people, who are kept in extreme poverty only to fatten the pocketbooks of selfish executives. Somewhere from the lower ranks, often the mailroom, an intelligent, handsome protagonist emerges to expose management's greed and incompetence. Through superior intellect and cunning, the hero is able to topple the powers that be, take from the rich, give to the poor, and improve the lives of thousands. It's the old Robin Hood story told over and over again.

And it's a great story. The problem is it's almost never happened. Yet this story is so ingrained in our culture that people actually believe it. The truth is quite the opposite: business owners, corporate executives, and top sales professionals are for the most part the most straightforward and honest people you're likely to meet. After all, the market weeds out most scam artists and frauds rather quickly. There are simply too many people watching over business for this type of activity to exist for any length of time. It's nothing more than a myth perpetuated by the media.

There are a lot of false beliefs surrounding the marketplace. To give you a fighting chance at success, we first have to expose some of these myths and replace them with a good dose of reality.

MYTH #1: THE BETTER MOUSETRAP

We've all heard the saying "If you build a better mousetrap, the world will beat a path to your door."

This myth encourages us to believe that big ideas sell themselves. In reality they don't. Every product, no matter how good it is, is dead in the water until someone sells it. I can't think of a single product that was so great it sold itself.

Anxious, inexperienced entrepreneurs focus on product development and services, while experienced businesspeople focus their attention on sales. The most essential requirement for success in any field is sales skills. And yet, sales training is overlooked in nearly every industry. Less than 5 percent of full-time salespeople have ever received training.

Several years ago, Nazila Alasti, founder and CEO of Jooners.com, spoke at the Symposium on Entrepreneurship at Stanford University. When asked what colleges could do to better promote entrepreneurship, she said, "Developing products is the easiest part of entrepreneurship; making the sales is the most difficult part. If you don't believe selling is difficult, just try to talk someone out of ten dollars the next time you're at the grocery store."

Sadly, most people fall for the notion that a "big idea" is just around the corner. They are waiting for a niche, a breakthrough, a new and unique product idea, or an invention that will revolutionize the world. They have the misconception that if they can just hang in there long enough, success will find them. Unfortunately, it rarely works this way. The truth is that waiting for success to find you is like waiting to be struck by lightning. Odds are it won't happen.

Let's face it, 99.9 percent of all sales worldwide are "me-too" products and services and are not unique. In fact, people are much more willing to buy improvements to existing products than they are to purchase completely new, innovative, and untried products or services. Your clients aren't looking for new products; they are looking for adaptations of existing products that better fill their needs.

The Ford Edsel is a great example of what not to do. In 1957 Ford Motor Company released its Edsel car to the American market. It has been called one of the greatest business blunders of all time. Before the Edsel was dropped, it lost nearly $350 million (about $3 billion to today's dollars), making it one of the most costly consumer product mistakes in history. The Edsel debacle was so costly that it nearly bankrupted Ford.

There has probably been more research done on the Edsel's flop than on any other product failure in history. While everyone agrees that failure to do market research was one the biggest contributors to the Edsel's demise, a lot of economists contend that the car was too advanced for the consumer to accept.

The car sported every gadget available at the time—power steering, power brakes, power windows, power radio antenna, and more. While all of these features are quite common today, back in the late '50s, they weren't proven, and so consumers did not feel comfortable with them.

Steve Jobs took the Edsel lesson to heart. When Apple engineers developed the iPhone, Jobs decided it was too far advanced for the public to accept. Two intermediate phones were produced to get the public comfortable with the features available on the iPhone. In all, it took eight years from the time the iPhone was first developed until it reached the market. Did it work? Apple is now worth more than Ford.

Personally, I feel the Edsel's failure had more to do with it being an ugly car than being too advanced for the general public. The wife of Henry Ford II chose the design for the Edsel. It was never test marketed. No one dared question Mrs. Ford's taste, and the rest is history.

If the Edsel catastrophe taught us anything, it's that manufacturers can't dictate what customers will buy. Products should be manufactured to appeal to customer wants. Market testing is a must.

Several years ago, I had the good fortune to speak with Jim Straw about this. At the time, Jim was considered the "dean of mail-order marketing." In his lifetime, Jim amassed a fortune of more than $50 million. Everything he touched seemed to turn to gold. I asked Jim how he knew which products to sell.

"I don't," replied Jim. "Fifty percent of the products I introduce to the market lose money. Fortunately, they lose only a little money, and the products that make money...make a lot of money. This is accomplished through product testing. If I offer the product to a thousand people and it makes money, I know that it will make the same percentage of profit if I make the offering to a hundred thousand people. If a product loses money in the initial test, I know to drop it and look for another product to promote."

MYTH #2: THE SELF-MADE INDIVIDUAL

Believe it or not, most people believe "luck" is the number-one determining factor in success. Urban legends about successful people support this nonsense. I'm sure you've heard plenty of success stories in which someone just got lucky, was in the right place at the right time, or just fell into success. The thing about all urban legends is, they are completely false. Success doesn't occur through happenstance.

Luck is nothing more than hope, and I'm here to tell you hope isn't a strategy. A lot of things have to come together in a short period of time for success to occur. Luck has little to do with it. Success isn't a gimme; you've got to put in the work. Even though the harder you work, the "luckier" you get, no one can do all the work by himself or herself.

Business, above all else, is a team effort. When it comes to success, there are two things I know. No one ever falls to the top of a mountain, and no one ever gets there alone. The surest way to fail is to try to do everything yourself. No one succeeds without a team. Find a mentor.

On May 29, 1953, Edmund Hillary became the first man to reach the summit of Mount Everest. It was one of the great achievements of the twentieth century along with Roald Amundsen, first to reach the South Pole and Neil Armstrong's walking on the moon.

There's more to the story than just reaching the top of the highest peak on Earth. Hillary would have never made it without the help of Sherpa guide Tenzing Norgay and the expedition support staff, numbering nearly four hundred.

Early in the expedition, Tenzing's quick work with a rope and an ice ax prevented Hillary from falling to his death in a large crevasse. During the final ascent to the summit of Everest, Tenzing—who had led most of the way—stepped aside just a few feet from the summit to allow Hillary to be the first person to reach the top of the world.

Edmund Hillary was a master at mountaineering, but Tenzing Norgay was better. At the time, Tenzing had more experience on Everest than any man alive, including three expeditions in the 1930s and a world high-altitude climbing record set the previous year. After the climb, Hillary repeatedly emphasized the important part Tenzing played in helping him reach the top of the mountain. On being knighted by Queen Elizabeth, Hillary told the Queen, "I could not have made it without Tenzing; no one gets to the top alone."

It doesn't matter if you're climbing a mountain or climbing the success ladder, no one gets to the top alone.

Ask yourself this simple question: "Could I achieve my goal faster with the advice of someone who has already achieved this same goal?" I think you'll agree that a good mentor can help you succeed at a faster pace. Not only will you learn new things from a mentor but also you will also be able to take better advantage of what you already know.

After all, a mentor's hindsight can become your foresight.

MYTH #3: THE OVERNIGHT SUCCESS

Otto Rohwedder invented the bread-slicing machine and changed the world forever. For decades every new and clever invention was praised as "the greatest thing since sliced bread." In 1928, the Chillicothe Baking Company began using Rohwedder's bread-sling machine commercially. It was an immediate sensation and two years later, in 1930, the Continental Baking Company introduced Wonder Bread as sliced bread and began to sell bread-slicing machines nationwide.

The media proclaimed Rohwedder an overnight success. While the bread-slicing machine was one of the great inventions of the twentieth century, it was far from an overnight success and certainly not a "rags to riches" story.

Rohwedder built the first prototype of the bread-slicing machine in 1912. It was destroyed, along with the blueprints, in a factory fire in 1917. With the need to get funding again, bringing the bread slicer to market was delayed for several more years.

Rohwedder's overnight success took sixteen long, hard years, and he didn't become rich either. He sold his patent rights for a small amount of money and for a full-time job as vice president and sales manager for the Micro-Westco Company of Bettendorf, Iowa. Not a lot of reward for one of the most notable inventions of the twentieth century.

Harlan Sanders and his wife drove around the country with a pressure cooker for nine years before he sold his prize recipe, which was then franchised into Kentucky Fried Chicken.

A more recent example of the overnight success myth is comedian Jim Carrey's rocketing to fame. In 1994, *Ace Ventura: Pet Detective, The Mask,* and *Dumb and Dumber* all became box office hits, grossing more than $700 million. Carrey had seemingly come out of nowhere to reach the pinnacle of Hollywood success.

As a young boy, Carrey dreamed of becoming a comedian. Times were tough. His father lost his job, and the family was forced to live out of a van parked on a relative's lawn. Jim went to school and worked eight hours each evening as a janitor in an old tire factory, all the while practicing his jokes. The first time he appeared at Toronto's Yuk Yuk Club, he was booed off the stage.

Still, Carrey was relentless in his efforts to become a successful comedian. He dropped out of high school and moved to Los Angeles to pursue a full-time career as a comedian. It took him only eleven years of practicing his jokes every day to reach success.

Our media romances overnight success because that's what we want. You seldom hear about the failures it takes to gain the experience necessary to build a successful business. Business isn't easy. What appears to be overnight success is usually the accumulation of thousands of hours of hard work.

Let's remember that business isn't for sprinters—it's for long-distance runners.

Today, people are more reluctant than ever to work for success. They not only want instant success but also demand it. Recently I spoke in front of a group of 120 incoming college freshmen. I asked them what exactly it was they wanted. The response was almost universal.

"I want a lot of money, I want it fast, and I don't want to have to work hard for it."

The Internet fuels the desire for fast money with its seemingly endless get-rich-quick schemes.

MYTH #4: INTERNET MARKETING LEVELS THE PLAYING FIELD

Everyone is trying to get aboard the Internet gravy train nowadays. And the web is responding with risk-free, guaranteed opportunities. The problem is this: The Internet is not a business—it's a medium. It's a way to distribute information and connect with potential clients.

I believe every business should have an Internet presence. You're leaving a lot of potential sales on the table without one. However, counting on the Internet alone to drive your business almost always spells disaster. Nineteen out of twenty people who market exclusively on the Internet lose their proverbial backsides every month.

The ever-expanding reach of the Internet now gives entrepreneurs the opportunity to expand their business beyond borders and reach hundreds of millions. Is it any wonder why today's would-be entrepreneurs rush to the web? Unfortunately, most websites are never seen and are little more than expensive business cards. Those that *are* seen are—for the most part—opened, closed, and mercifully forgotten.

There are lots of opinions on how to make money on the web. You can hardly log on without someone trying to sell you the latest and greatest success system, product-development plan, or launch blueprint. There are "Five Steps to Five Figures," "Seven Steps to Seven Figures," and everything in between, all guaranteed to make us rich. I even had one fellow guarantee me that if I gave him $7,500 he would increase my net worth by $100,000 within the next twelve months.

Well, sure, okay. But, hey, I didn't buy it.

It's best to view the Internet as a fantastic connection machine. It won't be of much use to you, however, if you fail to use it properly. The greatest benefit of the Internet is that it allows us to develop and build relationships with people whom we otherwise wouldn't be able to reach.

Most major corporations have advertising budgets in the millions of dollars. How on earth do you think a website would put you on a level playing field with that?

Ninety-eight percent of these Internet business schemes are nothing more than a bunch of crap and not worth the price, even if they gave them away for free. Most are written by well-meaning entrepreneurs who are more interested in making a buck than in helping others succeed. By and large, these people lack legitimate business experience and miss the most important part of business, that being the art of sales.

They brag about six-figure systems, when in reality a six-figure sales figure is considered by most sales professionals to be a slow week. It seems every one of these gurus is trying to outdo the others. Some of them are even trying to outdo their own latest product or system.

In this book I'm going to show you the principles that top salespeople use to get clients. It's important that you understand these principles prior to contacting clients. There's nothing worse than finally getting in front of a big client, only to destroy your chances due to the lack of proper sales skills. In addition, we'll discuss in detail what actions you need to take to earn their business.

Truthfully, any action is better than no action. I worked with a young sales rep for several years. He thought he was good at selling, but in the eight years I worked with him I hadn't seen him make a single sale. Sure, he took a few orders and made deliveries, but he never sold much. He had a hefty salary, a company vehicle, a company cell phone, and a monthly performance bonus. Still, he complained constantly about not having enough money. Basically, he had business cards that had *sales* printed on them, and he must have figured that was enough. What few hours he worked a day were spent making deliveries or just waiting around for a customer to find him.

Once he came up to me and asked very seriously what I thought he could do to make more money.

"You're in sales," I said. "As far as I know, there's only one way to make more money and that's to sell more."

"I take care of my clients and my sales figures have been consistent since I started here," he protested.

"You're right," I said, "but your sales have never increased and you have yet to bring in a new client to the business."

"Just tell me what I need to do, and I'll do it," he snapped angrily.

"How about if I give you a list of potential clients you can call on?" I answered. "If you call five of them a day, within a week you'll have at least one new client. If you do it for a month, you'll have four new clients and that'll get someone's attention."

He agreed and I left the room for a few minutes. When I returned, I handed him a copy of the Yellow Pages.

"Here's a list of every business in town," I said. "Stop the pity party and start calling."

As far as I know he never made a single call. He's still waiting and still whining about how much he's not making. He's not alone. This is exactly what 95 percent of salespeople do daily.

The problem was that there weren't any consequences in this company for lack of action. The company paid monthly bonuses. These were based on the entire company's sales and shared equally among the employees. About half of the employees worked their tails off and the other half coasted, reaping the benefits of others' work.

Rarely will a person make a good effort if there aren't consequences involved. These consequences can be either rewards or punishment. If the same results are achieved either through hard work or doing nothing, most people will opt for doing nothing.

Without consequences, we create a workforce made up primarily of deadweight. Nothing sinks a boat faster than deadweight.

The marketplace rewards only effort. Do nothing at your own peril.

"The man who complains about how the ball bounces is usually the one who dropped it."—Lou Holtz

So many people do nothing at all because they are too afraid of doing the wrong thing.

You're going to make mistakes. Everyone does. It generally takes two to five years for a business relationship to become profitable. That time is going to pass, whether you work on your business or not. Do you want your sales to go through the roof? Then get off your duff and get out there and start talking to people.

It's always too late to wait but never too late to start.

There's a lot of wasted opportunity out there just waiting to be seized. We're seeing an increased interest in business ownership. Seventy percent of people surveyed expressed a desire to own their own business. In any given year there are approximately one million new business start-ups in America. Most of these businesses offer good product for a fair price, but, sadly, most of these businesses will fail within five years. We have found that the businesses that succeed follow a proven sales model, while the businesses that fail often leave their sales to chance.

I wouldn't want to leave my odds of catching a fish to chance, and I'm not about to leave my business to chance either. I don't want you to become a statistic. I want you to be successful. I don't want you to just sit in the boat; I want you to catch big fish.

Chapter 2

● ● ●

BECOMING A FISHER OF PEOPLE

At a very young age, my goals were simple. Hammer fish, any fish. It didn't matter which species of fish or which bait I used. I just wanted to catch a lot of fish. I was always ready to bend a rod.

I was required to attend both school and church. The only valid excuse for skipping either was fishing, and I missed as much school as I possibly could without repeating a grade.

When I was a little fella, about eight or nine, my father scraped together enough money to buy a fishing boat. Every Sunday morning, Dad would drag my brothers and me out of bed before sunup to go fishing. To my father, fishing wasn't just recreation; it was art. Dad firmly believed that the most important lessons in life were learned with a fishing rod in your hands, and these trips became an important part of my education.

When the fishing was good, these trips were very exciting. When the fishing slowed down, these trips were as boring as all get-out. It was during these slow times that Dad would impart his wisdom to us. At the time, I thought Dad's lessons – keep your line in the water, don't bully a fish, and give them what they want - were directly related to fishing, but later on I realized they translated to important lessons in living.

It wasn't until I years later that I realized that most of what I know about sales and business success I've learned with a fishing rod in my hands.

Most people start a business and wait for the customer to find them. They buy a few ads and build a website, but mostly they wait. This is akin to buying a fishing boat, hitting the water without a rod and reel, and waiting for the fish to jump in the boat. It might happen, but chances are it won't.

Like many of you, I come from humble beginnings. I was raised in the logging and mining villages of the Idaho panhandle. Back then it was one of the most impoverished regions of the United States. Only a few sections of Appalachia had a lower average household income. We were officially lower middle class, which is a nice way of saying we were poor. We didn't realize we were poor, however, because everyone in the community was in the same boat. Most of our neighbors didn't know where their next meal was coming from or where they were going to scrape together next month's rent. The entire community was suffering from perpetual recession.

My father worked at the local service station during the day and ran the projector at the movie theater at night. My mother was a seamstress, mending and sewing clothes for extra income. I remember Mom searching through her purse for spare change, hoping to find enough to buy hamburger to feed a family of eight.

Our family had it better than most because Mom raised a big garden, and she canned both fruit and vegetables each fall. Dad hunted and fished to add some protein to our diet. Though we always got by, I can still remember the fear that we might not. Sadly, I'm seeing a lot of families reliving this same old money struggle nowadays.

In my youth, life was simpler than it is today. There were few houses, few roads, and a lot fewer people. In the three decades following World War II, American industry was king. More than 50 percent of the products exported globally were manufactured here in America.

Industrial jobs paid terrific wages, giving employees enough money to afford a house, a couple of cars, and the ability to send their kids to college. In addition, there was health insurance and wonderful retirement plans.

The security of an industrial job was too hard for me to resist. I gave up my dream of business ownership and took the bait. Overnight, my job in industry increased my income threefold and I was making more money than 80 percent of the business owners in town. I was living the "American Dream."

Gradually, the American Dream became a nightmare. US industry was no longer able to compete with foreign manufacturers, and it began downsizing and closing factories. Within fifteen years, 32 percent of the manufacturing jobs in this country were lost. Like a lot of Americans, I lost my job, my retirement, my insurance, and my house. Many of you have faced similar challenges and understand how terrifying it is see your entire life being ripped away from you.

Fortunately for me, the timber industry collapsed early in the recession of the 1970s, and I entered into sales in the middle of the greatest economic growth period the world has ever seen.

The 1990s were a sea of business opportunity. People had money and were spending it freely. All you had to do was row your boat out into that sea and wait for the fish to jump into your boat. There were plenty of fish to go around; you could pick and choose whom you sold to.

Shortly after the 2008 recession, everything changed. Not only did the fish stop jumping into my boat, they were getting darn hard to find and swimming away as fast as possible. The bait I had used last year wasn't working this year. I had to learn completely new skills and tactics. No longer could I wait for the fish to come to me; I had to go find the fish.

I began interviewing hundreds of the very best sales professionals in the world. I needed to know how things were sold. But the more questions I asked, the more confused I became.

I soon realized the majority of top sales professionals have no idea of why they are successful. When I got advice, it didn't jibe with my personal experience. I needed answers, I wanted consistency, and I wasn't getting either.

My sales career was spiraling downward. I was working harder than ever and barely keeping my head above water. I was afraid my epitaph would read "Beware! This could happen to you."

One evening I ran into Tyler Frazer, a salesperson whom I had worked with in the past in a local restaurant. Tyler was outstanding at both selling and fishing. He had been hounding me for years to take him steelhead fishing.

While everyone else's business was faltering in the weak economy, Tyler's was growing by leaps and bounds. He had just signed a $4 million contract with one of his clients. I was desperate to know what he was doing and suggested we should take a fishing trip together in the near future. Tyler had never fished the big rivers of the Pacific Northwest and was excited to go. My plan was to take a fishing vacation with Tyler and mix a little learning in with relaxation.

Throughout the trip I kept asking Tyler about sales and he kept changing the subject to fishing. Eventually, little snippets of information came forward.

"Fishermen find their dinner by finding their dinner's dinner. A salesperson does pretty much the same thing." Tyler said. "He finds out which products the client is buying and then provides those products."

"I've always thought sales is a lot like fishing," Tyler added. "Quit waiting for the phone to ring and get out there and stay in front of your prospects. If your hook isn't in front of the fish, he or she will be and they'll be catching your fish."

The most effective way to sell any product or service is a face-to-face meeting. It's ten times more effective than any other method of contact.

A personal phone call is next in effectiveness. After that comes direct mail and last is an e-mail message. Top sales professionals try to spend 50 percent of their time directly in front of their clients, and you should too. After all, if your client is talking to you, he or she is not talking with your competition.

Waiting for the phone to ring is like fishing in the boat.

Even though fishing and selling are completely different activities, the way we approach each is very similar. Let's say you were going to fish a new lake. You'd want to know as much as you could about that lake before you went, wouldn't you? You'd probably read everything you could about the lake and seek the advice of the local fishing experts.

At the very least you'd want to be able to answer the following questions:

* What fish can be found in the lake?
* Where in the lake can you find the biggest fish?

* What are the big fish biting on?
* What special tactics are working now?

Likewise, in business you'd like to be able to answer these questions:

* Who's buying my product or service?
* Where are these customers located?
* What other products are these customers currently buying?
* What problems are these customers currently facing?
* How am I going to reach these customers?

Failure to thoroughly investigate a market before doing business in it is one of the most common mistakes made in sales.

About this time I had the unique opportunity of working with two regional sales managers from the same international corporation. These two fellows sold the same products to similar industries and had nearly identical sales records. The only difference I could see between the two was the way they presented the product.

The West Coast manager gave a presentation detailing all the benefits and features of the product. He used a lot of slides, graphs, and product comparisons, and he provided predictable results. His counterpart, the East Coast manager, had none of this in his presentations. He simply said, "I don't know how it works; I just know it works."

Even though their presentations seemed as different as day and night, their sales strategies were identical. They depended on their relationships with their clients and the reputation of their products to do the selling for them. This explains why Bill and Bob could achieve the same results. They had developed a relationship with their clients based on trust. Developing trust in a sales environment goes further than either product quality or performance.

With this in mind, I began to follow a path very different from that of most salespeople. Instead of depending on the benefits of my products to do the selling, I decided to focus on relationship building with potential clients.

Once I had developed these relationships, I was able to ask clients what motivated them to buy from certain salespeople. I expected their answers to center on price and quality. But what I got was completely different. They too were more concerned with business principles and relationships than anything else.

Relationship was the key, but what traits in a salesperson were necessary to build a proper business relationship?

I began to take a new look at all the successful sales professionals I knew. I saw, over and over, the same seven characteristics at work. Highly successful salespeople shared certain traits. There was no "magic formula" for success—I can't overstate that. But successful sales professionals draw from a common set of traits, which make them more likely to succeed.

THE TRAITS OF TOP SALESPEOPLE
MODEST

Successful salespeople are not pushy and egotistical. They are modest and humble. They don't exaggerate the capabilities of their products or services. Furthermore, the buyers I spoke with claim that salespeople who are bold, brazen, or full of bravado alienate far more customers than they win over.

CURIOUS
Successful salespeople hunger for knowledge. They study sales and continuously improve their sales strategies. They show serious interest in their clients' businesses and want to help their clients become more successful. They aren't afraid to ask difficult and uncomfortable questions to close gaps in sales situations.

CONSCIENTIOUS
Successful salespeople are responsible and reliable. They show up to meetings on time and deliver goods when promised. They take their jobs very seriously and feel deeply responsible for the results their clients attain.

COMFORTABLE
Successful people are comfortable in their own skin. They don't embarrass easily and are willing to share their failures along with their successes. They view complaints as constructive criticism. They bring their authentic selves to the sales process.

POSITIVE
Top salespeople aren't discouraged easily. They look for the positive in every situation. They don't take "no" personally and easily bounce back from losses and move on to the next opportunity.

GOAL-ORIENTED
Successful salespeople are fixated on achieving their goals and measure their performance continuously. They are more concerned with how their products fit the customer's needs than the sale itself.

NOT BROWNNOSING

One of the most surprising traits of top salespeople is that they are not flatterers. Sometimes your prospect may need his ego fed, but if he's a Big Fish with his hands on a big purse, flattery is a waste of time, because his ego is already stuffed. Successful salespeople treat their clients as true friends. They don't feel the need to bring donuts or gifts to win business.

Actually, bringing gifts or freebies to clients only weakens your position as a salesperson. You'll be viewed as a subordinate, a scavenger begging for business and not as a trusted friend and consultant.

Take a little time to reflect on these traits. Ask yourself, Which of these traits are my strong points and which I need to work on.

Chapter 3

GETTING OUR HEADS ON STRAIGHT

"SETTING THE FOUNDATION"

At the beginning of my fishing career, my results were less than what I expected. (Translation: I wasn't catching any fish.) I was under the misguided belief that I could fish where I wanted, with whatever tackle I wanted. I thought if I just hung in there long enough a big fish would eventually find me. It never happened.

Finally, I smartened up and realized that fishing was about the fish and not about the person doing the fishing.

I'm of Czechoslovakian descent. So naturally, I like to eat sauerkraut and spare ribs. Fish don't. We all know it would be foolish to try to catch a fish with sauerkraut. We're better off giving them something they want—like worms.

I'm always amazed at the number of salespeople who miss this simple concept. They spend their time trying to force a customer to buy the products they want to sell and never take the time to find out what it is the customer really wants.

Now and then it's nice to get a good dose of reality to shed some light on the overwhelming sense of denial that permeates our belief in the sales process.

Our world changes at a dizzying pace, and the marketplace changes with it. Products improve. Distribution and delivery advances. Technology has made connecting with prospects and clients easier than ever.

Today, consumers expect more from the products they purchase: multifunctional, multi-use, and long lasting. No longer do consumers merely accept what's available. They demand that their individual tastes be met.

When I was younger, things were different. Filling stations are a good example. Back then, gas stations had soda pop machines. Your choice was limited to Coke, orange soda, root beer, and 7UP. If you wanted water, there was a drinking fountain outside. Nowadays it's hard to find a gas station that isn't also a mini-mart, offering between three hundred and five hundred different bottled beverages to its customers. I counted twelve different types of bottled water at one station. I'm not sure exactly what the difference is between waters, but apparently the customer does.

Service stations have discovered that if they don't offer the customer his or her choice of beverage, the customer will find a station that does, even if it means paying a higher price for fuel. It's been labeled the "Goldilocks Syndrome."

I'm sure you remember the story "Goldilocks and the Three Bears." The first porridge was too hot, the next was too cold, and the last one was just right. The need to have our individual tastes met has expanded to all areas of the market. Today's customers are just as fussy as Goldilocks, and smart businesses are taking full advantage it.

Why do people line up at Starbucks for a five-dollar cup of coffee? Because Starbucks makes customers feel special and caters to customer taste better than just about anyone else. Customers are asked no less than six questions when they order coffee at Starbucks. What size of drink, number of shots of espresso, drink temperature, choice of dairy, flavor of syrup, and quantity? People love attention to their individual taste. No wonder Starbucks enjoys a markup of nearly 400 percent.

Big clients are just as discriminating in their requirements to have their tastes met. If you want to do business with the "Bigs," you should be prepared to give them what they want.

We've all been told, "Do what you love and the money will follow." A statement like this would be wonderful if it were only true. It sounds good and people like to hear it, but it's undoubtedly one of the worst pieces of business advice ever given. Too often people start a business simply because they happen to love a product or service and want to make their living selling it. They don't stop to consider who their customers will be or whether their customers will buy the product or service.

While I do know a few people who have started a business with a product and developed their clientele later, the vast majority of successful businesses develop their clients first and only then introduce products. In other words, they find people willing to buy their products before they enter the market.

We'd be better off saying, "Do what your customers love and the money will follow."

In business there is only one rule; everything else is a principle. It's called "The Golden Rule of Business." This rule is so important that it should be carved in stone. Every entrepreneur, sales professional, and business owner should read this rule at the start of every business day.

The Golden Rule of Business: "Whoever Holds the Gold Makes All the Rules."

I'm always amazed at the number of business professionals who violate this rule daily. They try to force people to buy products they don't want and can't use, and then the professionals complain about sales slumping. Your goal should be to make more sales, not to change the rule.

I've been fortunate enough to know several dozen self-made millionaires in my lifetime. They all have several things in common. They are motivated, have a good work ethic, and not one of them is in the type of business they thought they would be in when they were younger.

There are three things you'll need to accept right from the beginning. Big Fish are not looking for new suppliers. Most Big Fish are trying to reduce their number of suppliers, not expand them. Their focus will be more on reasons to disqualify you as a supplier than any advantage your product or service might offer. They'll want you out of their hair as soon as possible.

Secondly, they know more about what works in their business than you do. You're not going to teach them anything. They didn't get to be Big Fish by not knowing where and how to buy the products and services they need.

And lastly, they are already getting the products and services they need to succeed and are extremely reluctant to say good-bye to their current suppliers. After all, their current suppliers helped them to get to where they are today, and there's a huge risk in making changes in the supply chain. It's discouraging and most people give up at this point.

Fortunately, I don't discourage easily. There's nothing I enjoy more than taking market share away from a competitor.

You can fish with whatever you like, but you'll catch more fish if you give them what they want.

Most business owners, entrepreneurs, and salespeople spend way too much time trying to keep up with all the market changes. Top sales professionals spend their time on the sales aspects that have never changed. Sure, they use technology, but that's primarily for finding and following up on prospects. When it comes to sales, one thing that's never changed is the human element of the sales process.

Technologies change. Human nature doesn't. Customer buying behavior has already been established. You're just spinning your wheels trying to change customers' buying patterns.

Humans have not changed much physically or mentally throughout recorded time. Humans were just as smart five thousand years ago as they are today, and our decision-making process hasn't changed either. The way people make a decision often fails to match people's assumptions.

Understanding a little about how the human brain works will greatly improve your sales results. There are three separate parts to the human brain: the reptilian brain, the mammalian brain, and the neocortex.

The reptilian brain, also known as the brain stem, is often called the "lizard" brain because it functions in you in much the same way as it does in, say, a gecko. It's the most ancient part of the brain and controls vital body functions such as breathing, heart rate, and balance.

The mammalian brain, or middle brain, is often called the gatekeeper. It's the unconscious brain. All stimuli have to pass through here before they can reach the conscious mind. The gatekeepers are what some researchers call the four Fs: fleeing, fighting, feeding, and...sexual behavior. Before we can get our message across, we have to get past these gatekeepers. It goes without saying that we should be careful not to do anything that could stimulate a flee-or-fight response in the prospect. Satisfying the feeding gatekeeper explains why so many sales-people like business dinners and luncheons.

The neocortex is the largest part of the brain and is where our conscious mind lives. It is where learning occurs and is responsible for language, reason, imagination, and abstract thought. Most novice salespeople believe that appealing to a customer's logic and reasoning is how sales are made. Well, I have news for you; when it comes to sales, the customer's neocortex is not your friend. This is the part of the brain that loves to analyze information. If we stimulate it too much, the only thing we'll achieve is "analysis paralysis." Nothing kills a sale faster. We'll discuss ways to combat analysis paralysis later on in this book, but, for now, our interest is in the mammalian brain, where decisions are made.

"Decisions based on reason and logic"; this simply isn't the way things work. All human decisions can be traced back to emotions, supported by reason.

Here's a brief explanation. Inside the mammalian brain is an area called the amygdala that is responsible for emotion, value judgment, and memory.

Emotions support our long-term memories. We remember things we care about. We can easily recall every time we fell in love or got into a fight. But most of us would have a hard time remembering all of our high school test scores or even what we bought at the grocery store last week. We have forgotten these because we just don't care.

Long-term memories support our beliefs. The more pleasant or traumatic the memory, the more it affects our beliefs.

Our beliefs support our decisions. True or false, for better or worse, we base our decisions on events from our past. The more emotional the memory is, the more it will affect our future decisions. Keep in mind, experience isn't always the best teacher. *Experience* is the name we tend to give to our mistakes. It has nothing to do with knowledge or expertise. The more we try to analyze our failures, the more ingrained they become in our subconscious mind and the greater our chances of repeating the same mistakes over and over.

If you focus on an unsuccessful sales presentation, you'll dramatically increase your odds of failure. For this reason, we should focus our attention on the sales that went well and forget about our failures as much as possible.

Selling in alignment with the customer's decision process gives us an advantage over the competition. This pyramid shows how the decision process works. Every section of the pyramid depends on the section below it.

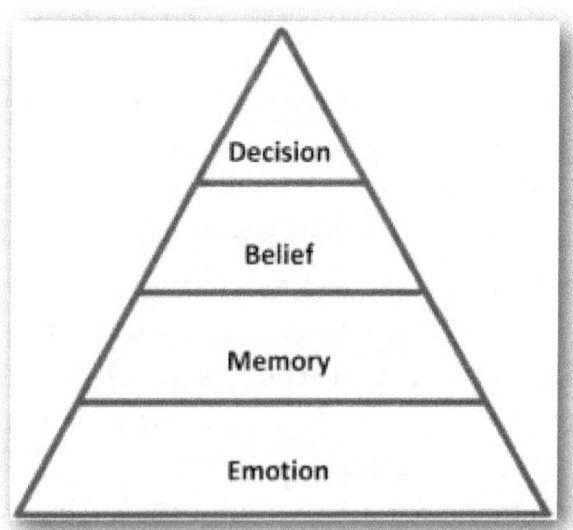

Beliefs are powerful. Once a person believes something, he or she knows it to be true. It's nearly impossible to change the person's mind. It's hard for people to unlearn what they've already leaned. Buyers already believe what they're doing works, and it's going to take some work to convince them otherwise.

That's why it's imperative that we create an emotional response in a prospect if we hope to change buying behavior. This emotional response can be either positive or negative, but without it nothing changes. For most people, a fear of failure will be a more dominant emotion in decision making than any positive emotional stimulation. The fear of what we might lose is more powerful than the unknown pleasure of what we might gain.

One insight into how emotions and tribal connections can effect change comes from a very unlikely source, that being drug-and-alcohol treatment programs.

We're all too painfully aware of the problems substance abuse has caused in society. Conventional treatment centers have had little effect in solving the problem. Ninety-five percent of people who go through these programs return to a life of abuse within a year. As one counselor told me, "It's easy for people to quit drugs and alcohol; it's almost impossible to get them to quit their friends. Shortly after release they return to their old lives, old friends, and old habits."

However, the Delancey Street Foundation of San Francisco has completely reversed this trend. More than 90 percent of the people who join Delancey never go back to drugs. Why are we, as sales professionals, interested in Delancey Street? Because if you can change the behavior of drug addicts, you can change anything.

Delancey Street has some advantages over other treatment programs. First, you have to apply to get in the program, and the waiting list is long. So, enrollees are highly motivated to change their behaviors from the start. Next, within days of being accepted into Delancey, its enrollees are given a job at one of Delancey's businesses, which include a restaurant, delivery service, and auto repair. Now we've added a financial motivation. Delancey works to break down old tribal units. Enrollees are paired with other enrollees who normally wouldn't be in their tribes. People from different religious backgrounds and different ethnic groups are roommates.

Here's where things get interesting. If an enrollee falls off the wagon, he or she is not kicked out of the program or reprimanded. Instead, another individual of the enrollee's tribe is demoted or kick out of the program. What Delancey capitalizes on is that people are far more willing to change their behaviors to protect or to benefit another individual than to benefit themselves.

Insurance companies have used this tactic for years. Remember those TV ads that showed a widow holding a foreclosure notice and saying, "I'm losing the house. If only John had purchased more life insurance…"? Advertisements that clearly show the benefit to an individual are, in fact, two-and-a-half times more effective than appeals to a group. This is where Delancey hits the ball out of the park.

No discussion about the human brain and sales would be complete without mentioning sex. If your product has any degree of sex appeal, you're well on your way to success.

Humans are animals and above all else we are genetically pre-disposed to perpetuate our species. There is no bigger rule in the science of life than evolution through natural selection. Sex is in our genes. We will die and kill for sex. There's no better way to get past the gatekeepers than to have a product with sex appeal.

A salmon willingly gives up its life to perpetuate its species, and the human need to reproduce isn't much different.

It's often been said that the best sales tactic is a nice set of hooters. That's probably truer than most of us would like to believe. Why do you think advertisers use sexy female models to promote everything from shaving cream to whiskey?

If you're like me and you don't have a nice set of hooters, you'll want to make your products sexier in other ways. We call this packaging. Your product should be clean, smooth, and streamlined and so should your packaging. It's not uncommon for manufacturers to spend more money on packaging than they do on the product itself. In selling, packaging beats product every time.

Packaging has as much to do with our dress as it does with the product.

My friend Jay Huggins puts it this way: "Dress in the same style as your customer. Don't wear a three-piece suit if your customers are farmers. Don't wear coveralls if your clients are business own-ers." He adds, "There should be only one slight, unnoticeable difference between your dress and your customer's. You want your clothes to be of slightly higher quality than the customer's. Not enough for the conscious mind to pick up on, but enough so the unconscious mind says, "He's one of us, he's doing well, and I want to associate with him."

Tattoos, piercings, and wildly colored hair are commonplace in today's society. Unfortunately, there are still far too many people suspicious of such "attire," or at least they are until they get to know someone. It's not right, but it's the way it is. You'll do a lot better if you cover your tattoos and remove your piercings when you meet a new client.

Several years ago I was working with a young man who was quite the flashy dresser. He wore his hair in a long, feathered mullet. He wore expensive alligator boots, designer jeans laced with rhinestones, and shirts with images of human skulls.

He worked long, hard hours and was very knowledgeable, but his sales were going nowhere. He was convinced his presentation skills were the problem and asked my advice. I pointed out that his problem might have more to do with the way he presented himself than with his presentation skills.

"Maybe the way you dress isn't resonating with your audience," I said. "Your clothes are very fashionable and your hair is well styled, but they might be more suitable for someone selling clothing or hair supplies instead of someone selling industrial supplies."

He was offended and retorted, "This is my style. It's who I am and I have the right to dress however I want."

Reluctantly, he cut his hair and started dressing more conservatively. Within two months his sales numbers had almost doubled. Who would have thought? About this time, he convinced himself it was his improved presentation skills and not the conservative dress that was responsible for his newfound success. He grew his hair back out and started to wear the rhinestones again. You guessed it—within a couple of weeks his sales were back to where he started.

I know it's been said before, but you can't make a first impression twice. Appearances are important. Most sales are lost in the first thirty seconds of meeting a client, long before the presentation. The salesperson simply wasn't dressed appropriately. People associate with and develop subconscious bonds with people who dress similarly. You need to dress as your clients do.

My second "a-ha" moment came not from a sales expert but from an extremely unlikely source, the renowned British zoologist Desmond Morris.

Morris's research gave us new insights into human interactions and decision making. Morris began his career studying the behavioral habits of fish and later he studied primate behavior. In the late 1950s Morris began observing human behavior and recording it in the same way he studied the behavior of wild animals. His first book on human behavior, *The Naked Ape: A Zoologist's Study of the Human Animal,* was published in 1967. The book was an immediate success and gave us a revolutionized view of humanity from the hunter-gatherer to the city dweller.

One of Morris's most interesting experiments involved an actor posing as a victim in need of immediate medical attention. Morris would study a passerby's behavior while the actor lay motionless on the sidewalk. People ignored the actor in urban areas, often walking around or stepping over the "unconscious" actor. In some cases, it took as long as three hours before anyone would stop and render assistance. Quite the opposite occurred in rural villages, where the average response time was five minutes.

Morris attributed this to our evolution from tribes. There are just too many people in a city for us to care about all of them. It would be a social overload. We view strangers in urban areas in a detached way, much the same way we view individual trees in a forest.

Morris argues that human beings have changed little in all recorded history and we are, in essence, primitive people living in a high tech world. The notion that humanity is a "mass of people" is false. Humanity is, in fact, a vast interconnected network of small tribes all woven together. Cities are nothing more than a series of small tribal communities living in close proximity to each other.

What's most interesting to us from a sales standpoint is the limited scope of tribal units. Some people are under the misconception that their Facebook friends, blog readers, and mailing list are their tribe. This just isn't so. Having too big of a tribe would be too much of a social overload for anyone. We can see the importance of connecting with people on a smaller social level. Otherwise, we'll just become part of the forest.

"The human animal has evolved over a million years living in small groups of no more than 150 individuals," states Morris.

While 150 appears to be the maximum number of individuals any person can have in his or her tribe, most individuals belong to tribes that consist of 50 or fewer people. These are the people whom you care deeply about—the ones you would go the extra mile for to ensure their success. And, in turn, they feel the same way about you.

People want to buy from people they know and trust. Trust isn't a grand gesture. It builds slowly over time, like a stamp collection or a savings account.

The size and scope of a person's tribe is limited. Yes, we can add people to our tribe. But, for the most part, every time a person is added to our tribe, another tribal member is removed. Perhaps the best way to understand this principle is to think about class reunions. We've all had friends from school that we swore we would stay close to forever. When we attend a class reunion, we realize that we have lost contact with many of these people for years. While they are still our friends, we are no longer as close to them as we once were. They are friends, but they have fallen out of our tribe. All of this occurs naturally and without conscious effort on our part.

Show me your friends and I'll show you your future.

Success doesn't fall into our lap; the choices and friends we make cultivate it. It's challenging to add people to our tribe but even more challenging to remove people from our tribe.

People tend to remain loyal to their tribes even when it leads to their own demise.

Addiction counselors understand this better than anyone. Addicts come out of rehab clean and full of hope for a new life, but this new life rarely happens. Usually within days, sometimes within hours, they seek the comfort of their old tribe (the friends who enabled their bad behavior) and the process begins again. It's easy to get someone over his or her addiction to drugs or alcohol; what's difficult is to get him or her over the addiction to his or her friends.

Everyone already has a tribe. Nothing changes until we change our tribe. Most people's tribes are built by chance or circumstance. However, top performers in any industry build their tribes with intent. This is what separates them from the average salesperson. My friend and mentor Brian Tracy puts it this way, "Your income will be the average of your five best friends'. The quickest way to increase your income is to make five new friends." I couldn't agree more. Now, how many of us could use five new friends?

Chapter 4

FINDING BIG FISH AND BUILDING YOUR NICHE

*B*usiness and fishing have a lot in common. Both require skill, are exciting, and give hope. Everyone who fishes wants to catch a big one. It's the same with business. If everyone but you are catching big fish, don't blame the fish. You're the one who needs to change tactics or location.

A wide, shallow stream flows through the forest. The water is only a few inches deep. Farther downstream, however, it settles into a large, deep pool.

Where would you cast your line? In the shallow, fast-moving water? Or would you cast into the deep pool that offers the fish both food and security? (I hope you picked the second choice.)

You can fish wherever you want, but if it's "Big Fish" you're after, you'll do better if you fish where the Big Fish live. Why waste your time fishing where the fish are *scarce? Ideally, you'll want find a niche where the fish are so thick you could walk across the stream.*

Unfortunately, most salespeople are scavengers and are willing to accept whatever comes their way. We are much better at coping than we are at improving. In fact, we'll spend more effort on ways to deal with a problem than on ways to fix it. It takes effort and a little skill to get in front of a big client, but it's probably a lot easier than you think.

When it comes to finding big clients, I'm always reminded of Lord Harold Samuel's famous real estate quotation: "'There are three things that matter in property: *location, location, location.*" That's as true for selling to big clients as it is for real estate.

Why do we feel we need to reinvent the wheel or come up with a big idea to reach success?

People want to know where the money is, where the jobs are, which products they should sell, where they can find clients. Truthfully, the answers to these questions are staring us in the face every day.

Sydney Miller was the placement officer for the University of Idaho for several years. Miller was always amazed at the number of college graduates who had no idea what they were going to do after graduation.

"They all seem to think there's some high level job in an exotic location with a fabulous salary waiting for them," Miller said, "when all they should do is drive around their own town and see what other people are doing for a living. You'll see the same types of businesses in virtually every city. Why? Because that's where the money is and those are the types of jobs available. If they would just pick an occupation, put their nose to the grindstone, and lean into their work, they would be successful."

The same principles apply when it comes to finding big clients.

The first place to look is in your own backyard. I say this for three reasons:

1. The only truly effective way to sell to big clients is face to face. You better have one heck of a travel budget if you plan on traveling to visit clients. Regardless of where your clients live, you'll still have to wear out a lot of shoe leather and burn a lot of gasoline to effectively reach them.
2. Ninety cents out of every dollar made in this country is spent within a one-hundred-mile radius of where it was made. More money is spent locally and not on the Internet, contrary to what some would have you believe.
3. The only way you can effectively utilize your existing tribe is locally. Big Fish prefer to buy from local vendors whenever possible. It's a lot easier for them to control product quality and delivery from someone locally than it is from some unknown vendor across the nation.

A lot of salespeople are under the misconception that they can simply march into the office of a big buyer or seller and show him or her product. They believe the buyer will immediately recognize the tremendous potential of the product, and they'll be off to the races. That isn't going to happen. In the first place, getting past the gatekeepers is nearly impossible. Even if you get past the gatekeepers, getting a big buyer's attention is even harder.

Not only are big buyers busy but also they're overwhelmed with dozens of salespeople throwing them pitches daily. If you hope to get their attention, you'll have to either know them personally or get an introduction from someone they know and trust.

We're going to start looking for new customers where every successful person does, among their existing friends and customers. Every time I say this, someone always replies, "But Jim, none of my friends can use my products." While this might be true, I can assure you that every one of your existing friends knows someone who can use your product or service. I say this because you are only six degrees of separation from an introduction to any other person in the world. Everyone has "a friend of a friend" who knows someone you need to talk to. Using your existing connections greatly increases your probability of success. I don't know of a faster or easier way to propel your business forward.

Most people find contacting existing friends for business introductions to be a little scary. We worry that we might offend someone. Don't despair. I am going to share with you a method that greatly reduces your chances of rejection and improves the cooperation you'll receive from your friends. The successful businesspeople whom I know used this exact method when they were starting their business, and you should too.

Mark Zuckerberg didn't create Facebook to build a $45 billion business for strangers. It was created as a way for him and his friends at Harvard to post pictures and comments and keep in contact with each other.

Christine Kane's first thirty-five blog subscribers were her friends and family. Her blog turned into a lucrative coaching business. Today, she is a much-sought-after keynote speaker and has more than forty-five thousand blog subscribers. It all started with her friends and family.

Your friends are your powerbase. Word of mouth is still the most effective way to gain credibility in any business, and your friends are more likely to spread the word about you than anyone else. You want your sales to go through the roof? Then get off your duff and start talking to your friends and acquaintances.

Start by making a list of all your friends, both past and present. Write them all down, even if you haven't talked with them in years. Don't just write down the names of people you think can help you. What's just as important as whom you know are the people *they* know. You don't know who might know whom, so start writing those names down.

Next, get their phone numbers and start calling them. This first phone call is to catch up with an old friend, and you need to be genuine in your desire to catch up. People trust their intuition, and if the person on the other end of the line feels this is a sales call, your battle will be lost before it has begun.

The conversation should go something like this: "Hi Joe, I was thinking about you and wanted to call and catch up. What have you been up to? How are your wife and your kids? What have they been up to? What are you doing for work? How long have you been working there? Do you like it? Say, where's your office located? I'd like to stop by sometime and see you. Or, better yet, let's do lunch."

It's important to keep the conversation positive and upbeat. Your friend will probably ask you what you've been up to, but resist the temptation to talk at length about your business. It's perfectly okay to tell them what you're doing, but keep your answers short and direct the conversation back to him or her. Say something like, "I'm more interested in hearing about what you're doing than talking about myself. We should really do lunch and catch up properly. When would be a good time for you?"

Eighty percent of the conversations should be listening to your friends talk about their lives, not telling them about yours. Take notes. Write down their physical address and their e-mail address. Later you can write down their spouse's name and their children's names. The idea is to gather as much information about them and their business as possible, not to sell them on your products or services. If you do this right, you'll have an idea of whether or not your friend can use your products or services. Even if I feel he or she isn't a good match for my products, I'll still do lunch with the friend, because I don't yet know whom he or she might know.

If I can, I'll do lunch with each and every one of the people on my list. If not, I'll drop by their offices and surprise them. I've never had a friend turn me away on a surprise visit yet. Don't bring any brochures or catalogs with you to this second meeting. It's way too early for that. Again, these are social calls and the conversations should be directed about them. If you show enough interest in them, they'll be more interested in what you're doing. When they ask about your business, tell them your business is going great and you love it and then tell them how much you enjoy returning a favor to those friends who are able to point you towards good prospects Give them just enough more information about your business to whet their curiosity.

The best time to ask for business is after your friend is comfortable enough to share with you some of the business challenges he or she is facing.

Ask, "What can I do to help you with your business?" Or, "Which of my products would best serve you?"

Notice I didn't say, "Let me know if I can help." Or, "Do you think my products could help you?" These questions can too easily be answered with a "no."

If I get a positive answer, the sale is all but made. If I get a negative response, such as "I can't use it or afford it," I'll say, "That's all right, many of my customers gave the same reply at first and now they're some of my most valued customers." Then I pause for a few seconds to let my friend think about it.

Then I'll ask, "Who do you know that might be able to use my products or services?" About 50 percent of the time I'll walk away with a name and phone number after just asking this one question. What will surprise you more is the number of these people who absolutely, positively didn't know anyone who could use your products but that call you back in days or even months with a name. Referrals are important. They shorten the time it takes to build trust and mutual respect.

Once I get a referral, I start the process all over. Again, I should stress the importance of not taking catalogs with you to this first meeting. Often potential clients will ask for a catalog. "Just leave your catalog and I'll be sure to look at it when I get a chance." This is a brush-off and their way of trying to get you out of their hair before a relationship can be built. Don't fall for it. Chances are they'll never look at your catalog and you've accomplished nothing more than wasting your time and your catalog.

Instead, when a potential client asks for a catalog too early, I say, "Sorry, I didn't bring any catalogs with me today. Next time I'm in the area I'll stop by for a visit and bring catalogs with me." This way I have at least two meetings with the potential client and double my odds of developing the necessary business relationship.

A few years back I was introduced to Rick, a buyer for a large international corporation, through a good friend of mine. We exchanged a few pleasantries and he immediately asked if I had any catalogs. I told him I didn't, which wasn't a lie. I didn't have any on me, but of course I had several on the back seat of my car. I wasn't about to be dismissed that easily.

I said, "Rick, don't you think we should get to know each other first? I'm not sure you would be a good fit for me, and you certainly don't know if I'm the type of guy you'd like to be in business with yet."

Rick gave me a big smile and we began to chat. I discovered that he had been on the job only a couple of months, that he had grown up in a small town not eighty miles from my birthplace, and that I had played basketball against his older brother. Now I had a relationship and a new client instead of a hope, a prayer, and one less catalog.

One of the best ways to gain referrals and introductions is to start small. Everyone wants to talk with the decision maker, and most salespeople look past support personnel. This is a big mistake. I've gotten some of my best referrals from the folks turning wrenches and pushing brooms. These people already have a working relationship with "Mr. Big" and regardless of their perceived "status," they have a much better chance of putting you in front of a big client than you do on your own. Some will eventually move up the ranks and become decision makers themselves. When this happens, you're miles ahead of the competition because you already have a relationship with them. Every relationship, no matter how minor or fleeting, has a value.

My childhood friend Mark used relationship building to land one of the biggest clients in the world. Mark and I attended the same grade school, high school, and university together. After graduation from law school, Mark and a law school buddy from Washington State University opened a small law office in Seattle. This was back in the early 1980s, and the economy was in the tank. Mark and his partner were struggling just to make ends meet. There was a surplus of lawyers and a shortage of clients to go around.

One day a young man came into their law office and asked if they would do some copyright and patent work for him. He had developed some computer programs and needed help. (This was long before anyone had heard of PCs or software.) There was only one problem—the young man couldn't afford to pay them and asked if they would consider doing the legal work *pro bono*. Mark and his partner could ill afford to do free work for anyone at the time, but they agreed to help.

Months passed and the young man was all but forgotten. Then he walked back into their office and asked if they were interested in being legal counsel for a new company he had founded. That company was Microsoft and the young man, of course, was Bill Gates. In the years that followed, Mark and his partner went from a small two-man law office to the largest law firm in the western United States.

You might think Mark and his partner were simply in the right place at the right time. But they were far from the first law office Gates had approached with his request for help. Every other lawyer turned Gates away once they found out he couldn't afford to pay. Maybe if Mark and his partner had been more established, they might have turned Gates away too. Regardless, they did the work without asking "What's in it for me?" and treated Gates like a friend. Friends often do things for friends without asking to be paid. They had no idea who Bill Gates would become. The lesson is simple: People who build great relationships treat every one of their relationships with the same care.

We find our niche in life not by focusing on our own needs and wants but by focusing on the needs and wants of others.

There are two types of clients that merit Big Fish status. The first is a client with the capability of buying and using your product or service. The second is a seller who is capable of selling your product. Of the two I prefer a seller. Getting someone else to sell your product is like creating a sales force you don't have to pay for.

Ask yourself, "What products are businesses in my area buying and which of these products can I provide at competitive pricing?"

Then ask yourself, "Who has the capability of selling my products?"

It's really hard to sell a product when you're not sure who'll buy it. I've developed a simple exercise that will help you to pick which products and clients you should focus your energy on.

Below I've included a worksheet you can use to match prospects with products. It's a good idea to fill one these worksheets out for each of your clients. It consists of two overlapping circles—a Venn diagram. In the left-hand circle, I write down every product

I can think of that the client might possibly be purchasing. In the right-hand circle, I write down all the products I'm capable of providing at a competitive price. I look at both lists and pick the four products I feel the prospect is most likely to purchase; then I write them down where the two circles overlap. Keep in mind that the center list is for products the prospect is likely to buy and not products you would prefer to sell. These will be the niches to build your business relationship in.

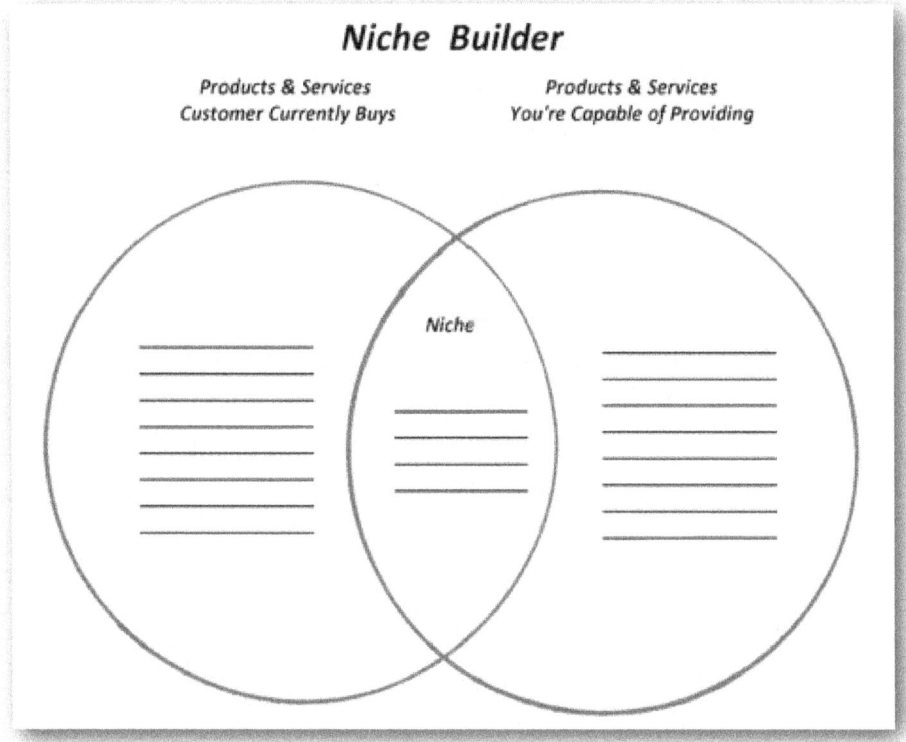

Starting a business without knowing whom you're selling to is like jumping off a cliff and hoping you can build a parachute before you hit the ground.

Once I decide to target a specific "big" client in my area, I'll ask my friends and colleagues if they know anyone in that organization or if they know anyone who might know anyone in that organization. People like to drop names of everyone they've met. It makes them feel superior. So don't hesitate to ask. It's a lot like dating; until you ask the other person out, the answer is no. Above all else, never leave a sales call without asking for a referral, and ask for referrals often. Referrals are the only way to consistently reach Big Fish.

Getting in front of a big client is a big deal. Big Fish have hundreds of salespeople trying to reach them weekly. It's akin to having a private audition for a movie role with Steven Spielberg. You're not going to get a second chance. You have to put your best foot forward from the get-go.

Try not to overcomplicate things. If your goal is simple, your plan should be simple. If it's not, something will go wrong.

If you've built your relationship and have done your research properly, it should be fairly easy to determine which of your products or services is the best fit for the prospect and you. Stick to that one product or service. Keep your presentation as simple as possible.

Regardless of how good your product is or how polished your presentation is, the odds are your initial offering will be rejected. Big clients reject proposals for a multitude of reasons. Maybe they have contractual obligations with another supplier or maybe they can't quite see the benefits of your offer.

Don't walk away. Don't let the prospect close the door on you. Ask, "Is there anything about your current supplier's products or services that could be improved on?" Let them know that you're asking as a way to improve your existing offering. Even if you don't get the sale you've at least planted the seeds of doubt concerning the capabilities of the current supplier.

If this prospect is important to you, tell him or her so. Say something like this, "I understand that my offering isn't a good fit for you at this time. It's important to me to be in business with you. Which of my products or services do you feel would be the best fit for you at this time?"

I try to ask this question before the prospect has had a chance to either look at my catalog or line card. I don't want to limit his beliefs on what I can do. Prospects feel obligated to answer this question and it triggers their thought process. It causes them to be curious about what other products you might be able to provide.

Often they'll ask for a line card and you can continue the sales process. But just as often they'll reveal a problem they're having or a product they're having difficulty securing. The very best way to get on the good side of a client is to be able to solve a problem for him or her. When prospects ask if you can provide a specific product, they are subconsciously committing themselves to buy from you. Even if it's not in your product line, never tell them that you don't have a line on that product. Instead, tell them you'll ask your contacts and see what you can do for them. Usually this product will be something that has little profit, and no one else wants to provide it. Successful people solve problems; average people run from problems.

Resist thinking about what's in it for you in the moment. Think in the long term. Do your best to provide the product. It's five times easier to sell products to an existing client than it is to a prospect that has never bought from you before. You might not make much on this initial sale, but it almost always leads to huge profits down the road.

My brother Bob and I used a similar strategy in developing one of our biggest clients. We got a phone call from a manufacturing plant looking for a small brass valve for one of their mills in Nevada. It was a critical part and their production was down until they could replace it. The customer had already called several suppliers and no one was willing to help.

After a few phone calls, we found the valve in a warehouse in New Jersey. The valve cost only seven dollars. We were expecting the customer to have the valve shipped UPS Red so he could have it the following day. Instead, he asked us to call the warehouse and inform them that a taxi would pick up the part within a half hour and drive it to the nearest airport, where he had a jet waiting to fly it to Nevada. I should have sold him two of them.

We made only a couple of bucks on that sale. Not much for two hours' work. Did the customer appreciate it? You bet he did. This customer is now doing more than a million dollars with us annually, all because we put his needs ahead of our own.

I ran into this customer a couple of weeks later and asked why he would spend thousands of dollars to fly a seven-dollar part across the country.

"Jim, I had the part on site and installed in five hours," he said. "Downtime costs me four thousand dollars a minute. If I had waited twenty-four hours, what would have that part have really cost me?"

Here's another lesson for you: Big Fish are willing to pay for results and trust those who provide results.

Once you've developed a relationship with these Big Fish, a whole new world opens up to you. Today, rarely a week goes by without some manufacturer or regional distributor calling to ask me to represent their products to my existing clientele. At last count, I had access to more than sixty thousand products that I can provide to my clients.

Chapter 5

* * *

FRIENDSHIP

There's a direct relationship between how much time you spend on the water and how many fish you catch. You have to have hooks in the water if you want to learn about fish. Spending more time on the water not only lets you learn the water but also gives you great insight into what the fish need.

On the Friday before Christmas 2012, I was eating at a restaurant with several of my closest friends and their wives. As the evening progressed, someone pointed out that my three largest clients had combined gross annual sales larger than the value of the entire annual agriculture production of California.

A puzzled and curious look came over one wife's face, and she asked, "What exactly is your job?"

I paused for a few moments and replied, "I have the best job in the world. It's 80 percent people skills and 20 percent other stuff."

Her facial expression became even more bewildered.

"Simply put," I said, "I find business leaders who can further my career. I make them my friends, I help them with their problems, and the sales come naturally."

Her face grew red with anger. "That's horrible, pretending to be someone's friend just to make money!"

"No one's pretending here," I said, "Business isn't Hollywood. It's for real. This isn't a fake-it-until-you-make-it game. You better be a true and genuine friend. You'll have to be there for them and have their backs when needed. If not, you'll eventually be exposed as a phony and you'll be gone faster than a fish can swim."

I added, "If *that* surprises you, then this will really surprise you. You'll never find better friends. Business owners and corporate executives are the most honest and loyal people you're ever likely to meet. They didn't climb the ladder of success by being flakes. For the most part, they don't ask for a deal, special pricing, or freebees. They expect to be treated fairly and in turn they treat their suppliers fairly."

Who says salespeople and customers can't be friends?

There's a lot of nonsense floating around these days about business and personal relationships not mixing. Actually, they go together like bait and tackle. Think about it. If your best friend asked to buy your product, you wouldn't overcharge him or her, would you? And if you were buying product from a friend, you would want to pay him or her a fair price, wouldn't you? Of course—you understand that your friend has bills to pay, and you wouldn't want to be a financial hardship.

Building mutual respect is an important part of any relation-ship. You must show your client respect, both personally and professionally. Too many salespeople are so eager to make a sale that they forget to show proper respect. For the most part, they remind me of high school boys on prom night. They're in such a hurry to score that they pay little attention to their dates' feelings or to the consequences of their actions. Is it any wonder why they seldom get second dates?

Doing business with a big client is a lot like finally getting a date with someone you've had a crush on for years. They're the kind of person you've always dreamt of. You want a long-term relationship with them. You want to see them again and again. Would you try to grab and grope them on the first date? No, you wouldn't want to scare them away. You'd take your time and give them a chance to get to know you and you a chance to get to know them. You'd show respect.

Certainly you wouldn't brag about your date and pass their phone number out to your friends. Treat your clients the same way.

Have you ever told a friend where your secret fishing hole is? Sure, he was grateful and promised not to tell anyone. Only the next time you went fishing, you found your friend already there with six of his buddies. The "secret" hole was soon fished out, and you were left looking for another place to fish.

I won't tell who my best clients are and you shouldn't tell me yours either. In the first place you don't need the competition, and secondly your clients won't appreciate your giving out their contact information to a half a dozen other salespeople who will be hounding them daily. If I did, I'd probably have to start looking for a new client.

What happens when you tell your friends where you're fishing.

The security in selling to Big Fish lies in becoming a member of their tribe. But first you have to accept them into your tribe. In Chapter 3, I discussed Desmond Morris's research on how people are more willing to render aid to a member of their tribe than to strangers. Well,' if you're not willing to aid a client in his or her hour of need, how can you expect the client's help in yours?

Last June I was running a booth at a trade show when my cell phone rang. On the other end of the line was Ron, a very big client of mine. Ron was in a jam.

"I need some gaskets to get the mill up and running," Ron said.

"What sizes do you need?" I asked.

"I already bought them from XYZ Company. They have them ready at their office, but they say they can't send them out until Monday because all their salespeople are tied up at the trade show. I know I didn't buy them from you, but is there any way you could break free and pick them up and bring them out here?" Ron asked. "I'm shorthanded or I would send one of the guys to get them."

"I'm on my way," I said.

I left the show, drove across town, and delivered the gaskets. There was nothing in it for me. In fact, it took an hour and a half out of my day.

When I got to the site, Ron was waiting for me. He apologized for asking for help and offered to pay me for the delivery, but I turned him down.

I said, "Ron, we're friends. If my car was to break down on the freeway and I called you to come and get me, you would be there, wouldn't you?"

"You bet I would," he replied.

"Someday I might need help, and we'll leave it at that."

Ron still buys product from the XYZ Company. But, guess who's getting the sales where our companies' product lines overlap? (Hint: it's not the XYZ Company.)

Harvard University surveyed thousands of businesses to find out where their sales came from. Businesses were asked what value their customers placed on various aspects of the sales process. The outcome was startling. The single greatest value to the customer was its relationship with its vendors. Relationships accounted for 40 percent of all sales, regardless of the size or scope of the business surveyed. Other survey results included customer needs at 30 percent, sales presentations at 20 percent, and closing skills at 10 percent.

Michael Corleone's (Al Pacino's) famous quotation from the movie *The Godfather* misses the mark by a mile. He said, "It's not personal, Sonny. It's strictly business." In business it's always personal, or at least 40 percent of it is.

One of the best ways to develop a relationship with prospects is to pay attention to what's on the walls of their offices. I learned this early in my career. I had been aching to do business with a large production company located in a nearby town. The problem was that Ken, the decision maker for the company, refused to see sales reps. No one, and I mean no one, could get an appointment with Ken. On a Wednesday afternoon, I dropped in on him at his office. I noticed he had a large display case full of belt buckles hanging on the wall. I could tell by his body language that he wasn't very receptive to my intrusion, so without a word, I went over and started looking at his belt buckle collection.

Ken came over and asked if I was interested in belt buckles. "Not really," I replied. "But I must admit this is an impressive collection. I bet there's a story behind each of them."

We started talking belt buckles. Ken told me a couple of stories about a few of his favorites. Toward the end of our conversation, I mentioned that the Moyie River Lumber Company had given me a belt buckle as a service award a long time ago and began to describe the image on the buckle. Ken interrupted me.

"I know the exact buckle you're describing," he said. "I've been trying to get my hands on one of those for years."

"I don't think I still have it," I said. "Gosh, I haven't seen it in years."

A few weeks later, I found the old belt buckle in a box of junk in the back of my closet. I decided to give Ken the buckle, not to gain business, but just because he had shown interest in it. The next time I was by his office, I left it on his desk with a note that simply said, "For your collection."

After I left the buckle, I was filled with trepidation. I had broken my number-one rule of business—never give gifts to prospects. My goose was cooked. I couldn't approach Ken again without him thinking I was trying to buy his business with a gift. So I let go of any notion of doing business with him or his company. Several months passed. Then one day I received a large purchase order from Ken along with a note to please stop by his office the next time I was in the area and to bring a line card with me.

Later, Ken told me that when he saw the belt buckle, he thought it was a ploy to attempt to set up a business meeting with him. When he never heard from me, he realized that the gift had no strings attached.

"What that showed me is that you're a professional. You showed interest in me that went beyond business," he told me. "Let's see what other business we can do together."

Pay attention to what's on the walls. See the pictures, trophies, the things they love. When you get prospects talking about the things they love, it builds trust.

Trust is the most important part of a sales relationship. Every customer you'll meet has been burned, at one time or another, and he or she is skeptical of entering into a relationship with a new salesperson. I don't care how good or affordable your product is, if the customer doesn't trust you, he or she won't buy it. Trust is the glue that holds business relationships together. Good business relationships are hard to establish. The take time and patience. In most instances you will have to visit a new client at least three to seven times before the customer is comfortable enough to buy from you. The good news is that once a trusting relationship is established, it's fairly easy to maintain.

Relationships are maintained through connection. I'm talking about personal visits and, when those are not possible, phone calls. Talk with your clients often, if for no other reason than if they're talking with you they can't be talking with someone else. E-mails and blog posts are one-sided conversations and a poor way to stay in contact. If you want to keep friends, you have to keep it personal.

My new friend Junki Yoshida likes to say, "Money makes you wealthy, but friends make you rich."

Yoshida immigrated to the United States from Japan in 1968 without friends or family and only $500 in his pocket. Yoshida's rise from rags to riches is nothing short of the American Dream. After a very difficult start in America, he developed Yoshida's Gourmet Sauce and eventually built a business empire around that product. Yoshida's skills at marketing and his ability to attract a big client are second to none. Today, Yoshida is the chairman and CEO of the Yoshida Group. He attributes his astonishing success to the relationships and friends he's made along the way.

"I've amassed a wealth of friendships in my life," says Yoshida. "If I had thought only of making money, my businesses surely would not have succeeded. True personal wealth lies in connecting with people. When you focus on friendship, money naturally follows. The year after I started my business, I participated in a charity golf tournament. Someone took pity on me and paired me with the then-president of Fred Meyer Corporation. We shared a couple of beers before the start of the tournament and were both feeling a little tipsy by the sixth hole. We had a great time chatting throughout the tournament, without mentioning a single word about business. Two weeks later, I got a call from Fred Meyer's buyer: "We've got a call from management to stock all of our 160 stores with your sauce." I was genuinely shocked. This is what I mean by focusing on relationships. I truly doubt that my sauce would have been sold at every Fred Meyer had I tried to pitch it on the green."

Yoshida, like every successful business owner I've ever talked with, stresses friendship as the key to his or her success. People want to be in business with their friends and tend to view their friends' products and services as superior to those of others. Not only are friends more likely to buy from you, they're also more likely to recommend your products and services to their friends and associates. Your business relationships often create new relationships. If you work closely with someone whom you've impressed, you will more than likely get introduced to someone else who will play an important and influential role in your life. Why not treat each and every business contact as a potential long-term friend?

Building relationships will increase sales and scale a business faster than any other activity.

Today, a lot of people try to build relationships and avoid the fear of rejection at the same time. They feel that staying in touch with everybody via social media is relationship building. It's not. Amassing connections with people you barely know will get you nowhere. There is no substitute for face-to-face meetings. Do you think Junki Yoshida would have achieved his level of success had he merely sent the CEO of Fred Meyer a catalog? If you really want to know people, ask them to meet for coffee so that you can talk more personally, one on one. It's a great opportunity to share ideas and experiences and to learn more about each other's story.

Don't try to maximize short-term profits at the expense of developing long-term relationships. Lasting business relationships don't just happen. It takes a significant amount of time and energy to build strong, lasting business relationships. They are an integral and necessary part of success, but people don't seem to want to put in the work. The secret is to treat your prospects as if they are already close friends. Always go into a relationship with an open mind and realistic expectations. Be who you are and accept others as they are. You don't put on airs with your friends, and you should be just as authentic with your customers. It's easy to create a false persona, but that's no way to start a relationship. Trying to be something you're not is akin to being a professional snake handler. No matter how careful you are, sooner or later you're going to be bitten.

Finding common interests with your client is an excellent way to build a connection. Be willing to do things with your clients that are not business related. Take part in community events. Play a round of golf. Go fishing. Join the Chamber of Commerce.

As in any friendship, we have to find a balance between giving and taking. Be loyal; let them know you have their back. Serving is the new selling. Serving and helping others builds trust like nothing else. But it takes two to make things work. So if you're doing all the work, you don't have a good working relationship.

A great way to build relationships is to share some vulnerability. We're all human and that means we all make mistakes from time to time. Believe it or not, showing your soft underbelly makes you more human to your clients and strengthens the relationship. (Use a little common sense here, though. Don't show so much vulnerability that you scare the client off.)

One of the most beautiful things about a good business relationship is that when you have your clients' back, they'll have yours. It's difficult to ask for help when you need it, but ask. It only strengthens the relationship. If it weren't for my friends, I would have failed a long time ago.

The sales strategies you implemented yesterday have gotten you this far, but they probably won't get you much farther. Effective marketing is no longer enough to make a sale. The days of simply presenting a product and making a sale are over too. Selling has changed from a rapid, impersonal process to a slower, personal process. We've learned that even if a person likes your product, he or she will not buy from you until he or she is convinced that you are a friend and are acting in his or her best interest. The most successful salespeople will be those who are most capable of entering into and maintaining relationships with their clients.

Building relationships, which are stronger than your competitor's is the most effective way to gain market share. The value of your customer will depend on two things.

* The quality of the relationship you have with this person.
* The amount of trust they have in you.

In a recent survey, businesses were asked what the primary reason was to change suppliers. The most common answer was that their current supplier wasn't paying enough attention to them—which incidentally is also the number-one reason for divorce. All relationships require attention and interest to be successful.

Simply put, if you're talking to your clients, they won't have time to talk to someone else. If you're not talking to your clients, I'll guarantee you they will be talking to someone else and you'll be in the position of finding a new client.

It's important to note that even the best of relationships will not guarantee you a big business deal. If the client already has a good relationship with his or her current supplier, you'll have to sweeten the pot a little. You either should price lower than the existing supplier or be easier to buy from. Ideally, you should be both. Being 5 percent lower in price usually isn't enough for a buyer to change vendors. The risk of interrupting their supply chain is too great. You can't win them all. Nobody ever has. If you dig hard enough, however, you'll find a niche with just about any big client you set your sights on.

Chapter 6

INTEREST

When the bite is on, it's a feeding frenzy. The fish will strike at anything. When the bite is off, you can still catch fish, but you'll have to discover what they're biting on. Even after you figure out what they're biting on, you'll still have to hit them on their nose with the lure.

Without question, the presentation of the bait is where all of your knowledge and mental agility are put to the test. You have to know the fish. I make it a point that if it's important to the fish it's important to me.

The first crucial step is selecting the right bait. After that, it's presentation. If your bait is properly rigged, there's a much greater likelihood of more hooks coming into play.

Selling is the worst way to win customers. The best salespeople always care more about their clients than they care about themselves.

Customers hate being sold to. They don't mind expert help when they need it. But much of the time they are not ready to buy, and one of the most irritating things is to have a salesperson try to get them to buy before they're ready. Unfortunately, too many people in sales don't seem to understand this and proceed to irritate their potential customers.

It's easy to resort to the old hard sell when it comes to products and services. We try to convince the customer that the unique benefits and features of our product will fulfill his or her every need. The problem is that when we try to push a sale, the prospect usually pushes back. I was guilty of this mistake myself early on in my sales career. My sales results were miserable. Eventually, I learned I couldn't dictate to the market. I had to let the market tell me what it wanted to do.

A good way to keep your mind on track is to continually ask yourself this question: "Am I a problem solver or merely a peddler?" When you approach your client as a partner in problem solving, all of a sudden the two of you are working toward the same goal.

Imagine going into a shoe store and seeing a pair of shoes you really like, but the store doesn't have them in your size. The sales assistant talks you into buying the display pair anyway, telling you that the shoes will stretch a little after you wear them. The next day, you have sore toes and a blister on your heel. You'll buy more shoes but probably not from that store. The sales assistant made a sale but lost a customer. Selling what's in your wagon without finding the right fit is bad business. In today's economy, we have to find a market and then adjust our organization or product to support that market. The market no longer supports a product; the product must support the specific market.

How do we get people interested in our products?

We don't!

Okay...we do, but not directly.

Building interest was one of the hardest lessons for me to learn. Year after year, I worked harder at sales than anyone I knew. I never missed a day of work for any reason. I thought if I sold harder, and wanted big clients more than anyone else, success would follow. It didn't.

The problem wasn't that I wanted success too much; it was that I had become too attached to the outcome.

When an opportunity presented itself, my focus on results often prevented me from taking the necessary actions to create success. I tried to force solutions, rather than letting things happen. It wasn't until I learned to lose my attachment to the outcome that I began to enjoy more consistent success. Once this attachment was gone, my success increased by leaps and bounds.

Novice salespeople miss a lot of opportunities because they're too busy looking for a specific solution instead of seeing the opportunities before them.

Too often, salespeople think the interest principle of a sale is when they give a presentation. Wrong. This is when we gather information to better match our products with the client's problems. This doesn't mean you shouldn't be prepared to answer questions, offer suggestions, or propose solutions. You should. Unprepared salespeople inevitably have poor results. We must be able to take advantage of any opportunity. This takes practice and a lot of it.

Remember, nothing is perfect in the sales world. Even perfect practice doesn't make perfect results. Business is too unpredictable. There are too many variables. We have to remain flexible. However, the lack of preparedness is a sure way to make a fool out of yourself if an opportunity is presented.

Having no plan is a plan to fail. Write down any questions you think the prospect might ask and be prepared to answer them. This is not to be confused with a sale script. I choose never to use sales scripts and recommend that you avoid them. There is no "one size fits all" in sales. Scripts are too impersonal and are easily recognized as a pitch.

**I wasn't prepared to answer questions;
may I just stick to my script?**

Before we can generate interest in our product, we must first determine exactly why the prospect would buy it. Only by carefully listening will we be able to understand what our prospects really care and worry about. Customers buy for their needs, not ours. Identifying the customer's needs is the first thing we must do before attempting a sale.

This is question-and-answer time. You ask the questions, and the client supplies the answers. It's hard to propose a solution if you don't understand the client's business. Don't be afraid to ask questions, even dumb questions. It is vital you have a clear and complete picture of exactly what the client wants and expects.

The secret is to listen without thinking about what we're going to say next. If we try to provide a solution without listening, we are only showing our ignorance, and we lose. We would be far more successful if we would spend more time listening to the problems of our customers and less time talking.

The one skill all top executives and salespeople share is the ability to listen and to listen intently. Listening is a skill, and it must be learned if we hope to connect with big clients. Take notes if you have to, but don't let your note taking interfere with your listening. Eye-to-eye contact is important. It shows that you are listening.

We need to listen with everything we've got. Careful listening elevates the value and quality of our products. When a prospect asks a question, we should wait two or three seconds before answering. This shows the prospect that we were listening and gives increased power to our suggestions. Our answers should be short and followed up with more questions. The more the customer talks about challenges, the greater our perceived value becomes. The best solutions to business problems don't come from finding good answers to the questions that are presented.

They come from discovering new questions. So, ask questions. Think of yourself as a doctor. A good doctor won't make a prescription until he has made a thorough examination of the problem, and you shouldn't suggest a product until you have a thorough understanding of your customer's needs.

Don't try to do too much all at once. Each of these principles should be taken for its own sake, and you should focus on one principle at a time. When you build relationships, you should be thinking only about building a relationship. When you're in the interest phase, you should be interested only in learning about your prospect's business. If you're thinking about solving problems while you're learning about your prospect's business, your focus will be diminished and you'll, more than likely end up missing the real problem. One small error, one missed detail, or one misperception at this point can mean the difference between success and failure.

Nearly every manufacturer I represent has a regional sales manager who periodically stops by to help with sales. It's all part of the game and if you want to be a distributor, you'll be asked to take these managers on sales calls with you.

It's enough to make you cringe. These are never good days for my clients or me. In the first place, the regional rep doesn't have the time to develop the necessary trust or knowledge of the customers to be effective. To my clients these reps are annoying at best.

For example: A regional sales manager for a material-handling manufacturer I represent comes to town a couple times a year. He's one of those pushy sales reps who tries to force clients into buying products they can't or won't use.

I suggested that he might do better if he slowed down and took a little time to get to know the customers before he jumped into a sales presentation.

"Show some interest in their business and they'll be more likely to show some interest in your products," I said. I even went as far as to give him a list of possible questions he might ask to break the ice with the client.

He nodded in agreement, gave me a twenty-minute lecture about his advanced sales skills, and assured me that he was an expert on customer relations as well.

As expected, our meeting with my client started out badly and went downhill from there. His idea of building relationships and showing interest boiled down to asking, "How are things going?" Even then he didn't wait for an answer, but immediately pulled out a ninety-eight-page catalog and proceeded to go through every page and product with the client.

Not only did we not make a sale that day, the client called my cell phone and instructed me to never bring that blowhard to his office again.

The number-one cause for failure in sales is the lack of properly investigating the prospect's situation and offering a solution too quickly. Years ago a group of researchers videotaped hundreds of sales presentations in an effort to determine the exact point where the sale failed. In every case, when the salesperson introduced his or her product before a full investigation had taken place, the prospect would visibly lower his or her eyes and no longer show any interest.

Discovering prospects' challenges is a difficult process. You can't just walk up to a prospect and ask, "Say, do you have any problems I can help you with?" If you do, he or she will shoot you a look as if you owe money and reply, "No, I have everything under control." Most prospects are extremely reluctant to admit that they're facing problems. The bigger and more successful the client is, the more resistance you'll encounter. Big Fish didn't become successful by not knowing how to best utilize the resources at their disposal. They often view such questions as a challenge to their competence. So don't ask. You'll have to be a little more subtle if you want to find what you're looking for.

Discovering problems takes time. Move slowly. Focus your attention on the challenges the prospect faces. Imagine that you are the client. Put yourself at his or her desk. How would you want to be sold to?

I like to start by asking about the client's business in general. Say something like, "I'm really intrigued by what you do here. Could I get a short tour of your process?" They'll almost always agree if you've built any type of relationship with them. Then ask if you can tour the process in reverse. This is called "reverse engineering," but it's just looking at a process in reverse.

Why?

Because viewing a process from start to finish makes common sense. First you do A, then B, then C, and end up with D. It's all completely logical. When we view a process in reverse, however, it's a lot easier to see where we could make improvements. The things that aren't common sense will stick out like a sore thumb.

Several years ago I was asked by a medium-sized lumber company if I could help it increase production by 25 percent without purchasing new equipment. I told its managers, "I doubt if I can find you twenty-five percent, but I'll take a look."

This wasn't going to be easy. The sawmill had been the most profitable mill in the nation for more than twenty years. It was an extremely efficient plant. The employees were the best in the industry. It would be an understatement to say they didn't like the idea of someone telling them their business. In fact, they laughed out loud at the idea.

At the time, I had three friends who specialized in equipment automation. The first two told me that increasing production without new equipment would be impossible. However, the third specialist dropped a bombshell on me. "Your aging equipment is only part of the problem," he said, "mills achieving the production numbers you're talking about also sort their logs to size." Now I had an idea of what to look for.

We began the next day by watching the crew load boxcars with finished lumber and worked our way backwards until we were looking at the raw logs. I could see immediately that log sorting would give them the biggest bang for their buck, but I kept my mouth shut. If I told them what I thought too early, they would overanalyze my idea and shoot it down. I waited a week and gave my proposal to the management team at their weekly production meeting.

I said, "I noticed there was a four-foot gap between the logs when they were presented to the saw section. This is to allow the logs to be individually scanned so the hydraulic cylinders can adjust the saws to accommodate the various log sizes. It that correct?" I continued, "My idea is to sort the logs to size prior to the saw section, thereby eliminating the need for the gap between logs. How much this could increase your production, I don't know. But I feel it could easily be a twenty percent improvement."

Predictably, I was met with resistance. People hate change. The log-yard foreman leapt to his feet and asked, "Do you have any idea how much work that would entail?" Whereupon he extended me his middle finger and left the meeting.

Fortunately, the owner of the mill was more open-minded. He ordered a test run and the increased production was just over 25 percent. That was twelve years ago and the plant still sorts to size.

Even if you can clearly see where an improvement can be made, resist the temptation to offer a solution immediately. If I had rushed in and given the lumber managers an answer to their production problem too quickly, I doubt if they would have ever changed their process.

Building interest in your products is what separates the wheat from the chaff in sales. The best way to generate interest in your products is to show concern for your client's challenges. Not all the people you're selling to will be interested in your products, but I can guarantee they're interested in solving their business's challenges.

Big clients are looking for partners, not rescuers. Don't be too eager to jump in and solve the first challenge the client reveals to you. These challenges might be only symptoms of a larger, more hidden problem. If you move too quickly, you could be missing the core problem. You want to be known for being thorough, not for being quick on the trigger.

Most salespeople tend to focus on challenges they are comfortable with and block out whatever they find confusing or mysterious. They use investigation to support preconceived ideas of what they want the outcome to be rather than letting their actual observations tell them what they need to know. People tend not to believe what they see but to see what they believe.

We must always remember that no two clients are alike, no two problems are alike, and no two sales are alike. Everything is in a constant state of flux. It is important to treat clients as individuals, not solely as members of a group. Each client has unique characteristics and will be different from any other you have ever sold to.

The ability to discern the core reason why a client would buy a product is the single greatest attribute a salesperson can have. Without this knowledge, we are just taking shots in the dark. We have to be crystal-clear about what this reason is. Sometimes it feels as if we're looking for a needle in a haystack. Once this knowledge is gained, however, we can tailor a simple presentation and our closing rate—in most cases—will more than double.

I'm no good at mind reading. If I were to take a course in it, I would flunk. Sometimes I can see a solution that the clients have missed, but most of time I must ask them, "What's the core problem you're trying to address?"

You must know what they want to achieve. Understand why you are asking questions and what you're going to do with the answers. Finally, you should believe in your solution. You must be able to look them in the eye and declare that they need to solve this problem. You must convince them that your solution is the best and that your approach will solve the problem.

People are loyal to their vendors, but they're even more loyal to brands. If you can offer them the same brand at a better price, you'll get their attention. Introductory offers can also be effective. You should take into consideration your customers lifetime value before offering a substantial discount. You're wasting your time discounting to customers that won't or can't buy repeatedly.

You'll need to show your client concrete and measurable results. Whenever possible, show the product and give a demonstration.

Test drives aren't just for car sales. People love to test products. Ask your clients if they could help you out by running a test on your product and give you a report on how it performs. Once they get their hands on the product, they assume ownership. If the product performs well, you can expect a purchase order. I've used this tactic on numerous occasions with great success.

Chapter 7

● ● ●

SIMPLICITY

Getting your lure in front of a fish is the easy part; getting it to bite is another matter entirely.

The biggest mistake fishing enthusiasts make is not setting the hook fast and hard enough. It's impossible to overstate the importance of setting the hook. Everything hinges on driving the hook point home. To become proficient at the hookset, we must first accept that it is a talent requiring experience and skill. Hooking a fish effectively and efficiently demands more discipline than merely pestering the fish to strike. If we try to set the hook too early, we accomplish little more than ripping the fish's lips. If we set it too late, the fish will drop the hook.

Simplicity is straightforward. If you do things right, less is more. Our products and services must help our clients to achieve their goals. Find the customers core issue and present around it. Remember customers buy results, not benefits.

A well-engineered product isn't one that has nothing else to add but one that has nothing to remove. Sales presentations work in the same way. A simple, commonsense offering will out-sell a mind-numbing PowerPoint presentation nearly every time.

A fishing buddy, who also happened to be a successful California trial lawyer, first exposed me to the importance of simple persuasion. Fred lost only one case in fifty years as a defense attorney. He later won that case in appellate court, and that's what interests us most.

"It should have been a slam-dunk from the beginning," Fred told me. "There were eight solid reasons to acquit. In the first trial, I gave the jury all of them. They came back with a guilty verdict. During the second trial, I gave them only one reason to find my client innocent. It worked. The jury was out for only a half hour and came back with a not guilty verdict. What I learned was that if you give people too much to think about, they become confused and it is nearly impossible for them to make a decision."

Short presentations are fast, exciting, and powerful. They make decision making easier.

I'm a slow learner and had to learn this one for myself. Several years ago, I represented a lubrication company with products that were head and shoulders above the rest. My presentation illustrated this. I made each prospect a loose-leaf notebook with bullet points, before-and-after pictures, thermal imaging, graphs, and data sheets. I even included my competitor's data sheets with highlighted differences. It was beautiful and irresistible. The only problem was it never really worked. I felt as if I was banging my head against a wall.

Eventually, I talked a client into allowing me to make a formal presentation. A few weeks later a vice president from the oil company flew out from St. Louis and we were seated in front of eight executives. I was expecting the VP to give a detailed presentation, but what he did was something altogether different.

The vice president stood and said, "Friction is wear. By reducing the friction we create longer equipment life. One way to demonstrate friction is to rub your hands together fast and firmly. Your hands will heat up. Now do the same thing with some type of liquid soap and see how much heat you can generate. Any questions?"

That was his entire presentation. No slides. No handouts. No graphs. Did it work? I had a five-figure order waiting for me when I got back to the office. After that, I changed my presentation. I threw away the loose-leafs. Instead, I devoted my time to discovering the core reason why the prospect would buy my product and presenting my product accordingly.

Our presentations have to be compact because people can remember only so much information at once. The longer a sales rep works on a pitch, the more likely the rep is to miss the buyer's core reason for buying. I'm not suggesting that you withhold information from your clients. I'm merely saying you'd be better off spoon-feeding information than dropping it all on them at once.

Ninety-nine percent of sales presentations are nothing more than hot air. They contain all the glitz and glamor of a television ad. They try to impress the client with how wonderful their company is. There are charts, PowerPoint slides, and forty-page reports, none of which are very effective or differentiate them from the crowd.

Don't make selling too complicated. Charts, data, and slides can make you feel important, but they rarely impress buyers. The more information we give clients, the more they want to shop around. This is true for both individual items and large supply contracts.

If we've done the proper amount of relationship building and investigation into the client's problems, asking for the sale is the easiest part. Simply repeat back to the customer his or her concerns, offer a solution, and say, "This makes perfect sense to me. What do you think?"

If you want to get a client's attention, jump right in and get to the point. Lead off with how your product will help him or her to achieve key goals. Don't start your presentation by saying, "It's a beautiful day" or "It's an honor to be here." You risk losing your prospect's attention before the start. Start with a "you" question. Something like "Do you want to increase sales?" or "Would you like to reduce costs?"

One of the best sales presentations I've ever seen was a real life "David and Goliath" story. The owner of a business with twelve employees asked me to help with a formal presentation. The competition consisted of some of the largest corporations on the planet. Many of them had hundreds of warehouses and thousands of employees. It looked like an impossible task.

Each competitor was allowed a half hour for a PowerPoint presentation and a half hour for questions and answers. The prospect's letter of invitation began "In an effort to reduce costs..." This was the core reason for the presentations and, fortunately for us, most of the competition missed it.

We began by slashing the business owner's multipage presentation down to two pages. Everything that wasn't about reducing costs was eliminated. We trimmed the number of slides down to a dozen. The last slide said, "We're Listening" and showed a colored graph illustrating the cost savings we had provided in the past year.

We were scheduled to present last. As expected, nearly every presentation was going past the one-hour limit.

When our turn finally came, the owner of the twelve-employee business hit it out of the park. The slideshow lasted less than ten minutes and, when he was done, only one question was asked. There wasn't any bragging about our products or service. We intentionally avoided any discussion of price, quality, delivery, or discounts. Our focus was on positive results the client could expect by doing business with us. Not only did we walk away with a multi-million-dollar contract but also we were asked to tour the client's warehouses to see what other products we could provide.

"Would you prefer the technical or the simple version?"

If we eliminate all of the fluff that doesn't work, what's left is focused, simple, and practical. You don't want to drown your prospects with data. The human brain didn't evolve to digest statistics and data. Don't get me wrong—data has a place, and that's to back up the client's decision to buy.

I'm often asked to give supporting documents. I usually supply a short synopsis of the product, along with a picture. It really isn't difficult to turn a ten-page technical report into two or three paragraphs highlighting the results you hope to achieve. I always include a copy of the full technical data or a link to the manufacturer's website. This helps to keep the customer from analysis paralysis.

A great way to make simple and powerful presentations is to use stories. As humans, we talk, think, and dream in stories. Stories are how we communicate with each other. Good stories are essential in selling because it's much easier for people to remember a story than a bunch of facts and figures. All businesses need stories. They're the fastest way to build connections with your customers. Stories are the best equipment you have for selling. Don't try to tell me that you don't have any stories. Everyone has thousands of stories unless he or she has been living in a cave.

Don't use stories to push a product. High-pressure sales always meet resistance. When we push people, they always push back. Present your story as a partnership in problem solving. That way, all of a sudden you and the client are working toward the same goal.

A good introductory story should answer the following questions:

1. What is the problem you solve?
2. What is the core benefit you give people?

3. How is your business different from your competitor's?
4. How did your business get started?
5. What obstacles did you have to overcome to make your business work?

In today's market, it is critical to have an "identity" if you want to succeed. You need to stand out from the crowd. To do this, you'll have to be your unique and authentic self; after all, everyone else is already taken. Imitating others will get you nowhere.

You can sell similar or even the exact same products as your competitors, but your story will have to be about you. Be sure to include what motivated you to be in business, the challenges you've faced, and the positive outcomes you've achieved. Warning: sharing your challenges shouldn't appear to be an attempt to gain sympathy. You don't want to draw people into a soap opera. Talking about challenges is admitting and taking responsibility for your mistakes, not a "poor me" session.

While everyone tells stories, few have mastered the art. We've all experienced the "blowhard" at a party who tells a lengthy story that no one is interested in hearing. This type of storytelling leaves people bored to death and running for the hills. What you want is a story that's short and sweet. An ideal sales story rarely takes longer than thirty seconds to tell—anything longer than that and you risk losing the prospect's attention.

Too often the novice salesperson attempts to build a story slowly and offer a dramatic solution at the end of the presentation. This might work for television and the movies, but it's an extremely ineffective way to make a sale. In sales, you want to get to the point fast.

Begin with the benefit the client can expect and work backward. We call this type of storytelling an inverted pyramid. This dramatically reduces analysis paralysis in your client.

I first learned about the inverted pyramid back when I was a journalism student. News reporters write stories in this format. They are obsessed with finding what matters most to the reader. The first paragraph contains what matters to the reader, including the who, what, why, and when of the story. The following paragraphs give additional information in descending order of importance. This way when an editor is pressed for space, he or she can chop off the last paragraphs of the story without losing any of its meaning. This formula is as effective in selling as it is in publishing.

Good stories are not innocent. They should be either directly related to your product or loosely related to the customers "why" for buying. Never bring up more than three benefits in any one story. Generally people have a hard time remembering more than three things at once. If you say more than three things about your product, you'll have said nothing at all.

Your stories don't necessarily have to come from your own experience. Telling other people's stories is often more effective because you don't come across as bragging. Instead of saying that you did this and that, you say so-and-so did this and here's what happened.

Stories need to show, not tell. The most powerful stories are ones that paint a mental picture, allowing listeners to fill in the blanks and draw the conclusion for themselves. Throw in a few specific details; they help fill out the scene in the client's mind. Details are like the colors on an artist's palette. Use them.

Several years ago I was attempting to sell elk-skin gloves to a manufacturing plant. The manager called me into his office and complained that my gloves cost three times more than the gloves he was currently providing to his employees.

He asked, "Why should I buy your gloves? Can you give me one good reason?"

I could have talked about the quality of the gloves, but instead I said, "Do you remember the famous dance team called the Radio City Music Hall Rockettes? Well, one cold winter's day the owner of Radio City called the Rockettes' manager into his office, complaining about a bill he had received for silk stockings. He suggested the manager that they should buy nylon stockings because they were cheaper.

"I don't think anyone in the audience can tell the difference whether the girls are wearing silk or nylon," the owner said.

"You're correct," the manager replied. "The audience won't be able to tell the difference. But the girls—they can sure tell the difference."

Needless to say, the Rockettes got to keep their silk stockings, and I made a glove sale.

Let's contrast the above story with the way items are usually sold. I would have said something like this: "These gloves might be three times more expensive, but they should last a lot longer if your people will take care of them. Showing your employees that you care enough to buy them the best will go a long ways toward keeping a happy workplace."

It's easy to see how an effective story can increase sales dramatically.

Just remember to keep your sale as simple as possible. Tell simple stories and offer simple solutions.

Chapter 8

* * *

HONESTY

Early to bed,
Early to rise,
Fish all day,
And tell big lies.

People who love to fish have been stereotyped as routinely stretching the truth. After all, nothing makes a
fish bigger than almost being caught.

However, not all people who fish are liars—only
the ones who aren't very good at it. Sales works much
the same way. The only sales professionals who lie
are the ones who aren't very good at it.

Simply put, it's unethical to put a spin on the facts.

Honesty in sales goes a lot further than simply telling the
truth about your products and services. It's telling it like it is.
Total openness and candor is required in every aspect of the

sale. While it's easy to say you practice candor in your sales process, it's anything but easy.

Clients are always looking for the perfect product, the one that solves all their problems. No such product exists. Don't try to tell your client that your product is the best. Everyone says this and no client believes it. There are advantages and disadvantages to every product. Most salespeople present only the positive aspects of their products and omit any shortcomings. It's easy to do since the buyer doesn't want to hear about disadvantages. This works until the drawbacks become a problem for the client. When failure occurs, and it will, the client will be more dissatisfied with you than with the product. You will be a liar by omission, and it will be nearly impossible to regain his or her trust. Keep in mind that it's a hell of a lot easier to explain possible problems before the sale than after.

Honesty helps speed up the transaction. It's a lot easier for the client to make a decision with all the cards are on the table. It's nearly impossible to get a positive response when the client suspects you're withholding information. What you perceive as a drawback might not be consequential to the prospect. Simply tell it how you see it. Trust that the client knows his business and is fully capable of making the best decision.

There's always more than one way to skin a fish. Even though I always attempt to reduce the number of buying options to avoid analysis paralysis, sometimes there isn't one best solution. At times like this, I offer two choices. It's okay to tell the client which product you prefer, but in the end the choice must be the end user's.

Practicing candor is the only way you'll ever elevate your status from salesperson to consultant. Candor simply means that all critical information gets to the client prior to the purchase. Often I get e-mails from clients asking for a product that, for the life of me, I can't see benefiting them. If you suspect the client can't benefit from the product, ask what he or she wants to achieve. If you still can't think of any benefit, tell the client so and why.

I've never lost a client by trying to talk him or her out of buying something that is not needed. In fact, such clients become even more loyal in buying from me and often ask my advice on products they're purchasing from other vendors. Both the level of my sales and the value of my advice increase.

**"When I asked for an honest opinion,
I didn't think you'd be
dumb enough to give it."**

Candor and transparency are key in retaining clients for the long haul.

There sure is a lot of lip service being paid to business transparency these days. Everyone seems to be on the "create a transparent culture" bandwagon. No matter what a company's official jargon is, true transparency is rare.

The goal of transparency is to build trust and open lines of communication. Transparency gets more people involved in the conversation. The more people involved, the more challenges, questions, and possible solutions are exposed. Being involved in these discussions is a win-win situation.

Transparency builds trust, but don't overdo it. I suggest you start small and see where it goes. Share short snippets about what you're working on, things you're learning, and updates to your products. Later you can include decisions about things you're struggling with.

Most large corporations require some degree of transparency with their suppliers. Not only do they want to know if your pricing is in line but also they want to know if your company is solvent and has adequate financial resources to meet their demands. In some cases, they'll ask you to open your books for examination. It takes a lot of time and money to set someone up as a vendor. No one wants to start looking for another vendor. This must be a mutually beneficial relationship for both parties.

Most vendors are offended when asked to open their books. Don't be. It means you've made the short list and they want to do business with you. It's the corporate world's way of saying, "Trust, but verify."

Connecting with customers on a personal level is crucial in growing a business that retains loyal clients. Two-thirds of clients choose shared values as the primary reason they remain loyal.

Although business transparency has been around throughout history, Jack Welch, the former CEO of General Electric, made it popular. There was a story floating around in which a sales executive got a meeting with Jack Welch. Jack walked in, shook the executive's hand and said, "Okay...so how can we make each other money today?"

I have my doubts as to the validity of the story. Frankly, CEOs rarely meet with sales executives. They have other people to do that. But I'm certain that's the directive he gave to GE executives. Welch insisted on transparency in all of GE's dealings. He believed that business had to be a win-win for all parties concerned.

Was he successful?

With Jack Welch at the helm, GE's value increased 4,000 percent.

The days of smacking the client over the head with jacked-up pricing are long gone. There's just too much information out there. When I started in sales, I was taught to keep our costs a secret. One lesson I learned a long time ago is the need to be transparent with your clients. I learned this one quite by accident.

One afternoon I got a call from a client needing a thermal imaging camera from a manufacturer not on his company's vendor list. He asked me to act as a third-party buyer. He supplied me with the manufacturer's part number and contact information. He needed the camera the next day.

I called the manufacturer and was able to negotiate only a 10 percent discount for resale. I remember the price being just over $5,000. The next morning, I showed up at his office with the camera and an invoice for $4,995.00.

He looked at the invoice and said, "This is a pretty good day for you."

"What do you mean?" I asked.

"Everyone knows that retailers have a fifty-percent markup. You made twenty-five hundred dollars on this sale."

I just happened to have the invoice from the manufacturer in my pocket. I pulled it out and handed it to him. My costs with shipping had come to a little over $4,600.

"Anyone who thinks there's a fifty-percent markup in retail has never turned the key on a brick-and-mortar business," I said. "I know they teach a fifty-percent markup in business school, but it rarely exists. There's just too much competition these days."

He studied the invoice and replied, "You really should charge more for your services."

Being transparent about my costs not only built his trust but also increased my sales volume with his company tenfold immediately. Never again did his company question me about pricing.

Research shows that customers aren't loyal to any one business, but they are loyal to the beliefs a company stands for. Share your business beliefs with your clients, and let them know that you're on the same team as they are. It's a great way to enhance the relationship.

A big part of honesty is owning mistakes. You don't have to take the blame for things beyond your control, but it's important that you take responsibility to correct them. Every product has failures from time to time. Even the best manufacturers can have problems. Nearly all of us have had a car recalled at one time or another; the products you sell are no different. Fortunately, how we handle mistakes is more important than the mistake itself. Owning up to mistakes and taking corrective measures will get you a lot further than pointing the finger and sneaking away.

Recently, I was faced with just such a catastrophe. I received a call from an industrial client complaining that some of the parts I had sold him were failing. I immediately drove to the site to see the problem for myself. As I was going through security my cell phone rang with another client who was experiencing the same problem. It was obviously a manufacturing defect. The bigger problem was that I had several thousand of these parts at numerous locations throughout the area. The nightmare had begun.

I called the manufacturer and had replacement parts shipped in overnight. I took samples of the failed parts and sent them to both the manufacturer and an independent failure-analysis laboratory. Then came the painful task of calling all my clients and letting them know that there was a possible problem. The manufacturer and I replaced more than three thousand parts within a couple of weeks. Loss in production to my clients was estimated at more than half a million dollars. Because we took full responsibility and quickly resolved the problem, the manufacturer and I didn't lose any clients. Oh, they weren't happy about the failure, but they were impressed with how we handled it.

The cost associated with fixing problems can be great, but the cost of losing a client is always greater. Whenever a problem appears, act to solve it. If you hear about a possible problem, let everyone who might be affected know there could be trouble coming. This way if a problem does occur, you will be the first one they call to help them solve it.

Complete honesty is a requirement for building respect and creating trust.

I want to end this chapter on honesty with a lesson on how not to play the game.

My very first full-time sales job was selling industrial tools. I had been on the job only a couple of days and made a presentation to a buyer for a large corporation. As I was leaving, the buyer told me he could sure use a cordless drill.

"I'll send you a quote," I said.

On my way to the parking lot one of his employees grabbed me and said, "You're straight off the farm, aren't you? He doesn't want a quote. He wants the drill for his personal use. It's just how the game is played. You scratch his back and he'll scratch yours."

"Listen," I said. "I'll provide you guys with the highest quality tools at the best price I can, but I'm not about to do anyone any favors in exchange for his or her business."

I don't know if I ever could have done business with that buyer or not, because I never let my shadow cross his door again. I just won't do business that way.

Over the years I've been asked to provide unscrupulous buyers from large corporations with everything from 49ers tickets to hookers. I turned them all down and recommend you do too. There is no way you can win at the bribery game.

I've seen a lot of these nogoodniks come and go. Mostly I've seen them go. Big companies will not tolerate sleazy business of this sort. If you ever get caught engaging in this type of activity, you will be banned for life from doing business with that corporation. This business is tough enough without having to constantly look over your shoulder.

Once I knew a piping contractor who had a bad habit of giving away flat screen TVs and rifles to gain sales. He had to raise the price of his products to cover the cost of his gifts. It didn't take long before a senior buyer noticed his pricing was way out of line, and she started buying from another vendor. At this, the piping contractor got mad and went to the company's HR department. He complained that its employees were demanding gifts from him to do business with them. He even had the receipts for the TVs and guns with him. The employees were fired and he was permanently removed from their vendor list. True story.

Years ago, when the market was strong and everyone was making money, big business had the tendency to turn a blind eye to gifting to gain contracts. When the market tightened, things changed. Participants in these pay-to-play schemes were removed from their posts and vendors were banned from doing any further business. The feeling is that if you can afford to give lavish gifts to gain business, you're charging too much in the first place.

In the long run, an honest person can make more money than a crook can steal.

Chapter 9

TIGHTENING LINES AND SHARPENING HOOKS

If I had only one day to fish, the first thing I'd do is sharpen my hooks. More big fish are lost due to dull hooks than any other reason. I have never seen a hook, even those right out of the package, that couldn't be improved with a few licks from a hook file. A properly sharpened hook will scare you. When you touch the hook, it should stick to your skin like Velcro.

The only way I know to outfish someone is to out-work him or her. You'll need to get on the water earlier and stay longer than the rest.

Sales is the only profession I know of in which you can create income at will, and there has never been a better time to be in sales.

More opportunities exist today for entrepreneurs and business start-ups than ever before. There is more money in circulation and more demand for products and services than ever. However, these opportunities will exist only for those who embrace change and are willing to learn new skills.

To become a skillful salesperson, you must be ready to invest in gaining knowledge in many fields, and sales is only one of them. Along with developing relationships and listening skills, you'll also need a deep familiarity with the products you intend to sell. To top it off, you must be able to back up all of this with personal experience. It's a lot easier to understand your customer's wants if you're a customer yourself.

Once you've gained expertise in your field, there are only three things keeping you from reaching your sales goals. They are lack of training, a lack of focus, and a failure to follow-up.

How important is training?

Nothing will kick-start your business faster than sales training. Sales training isn't a one-shot fix. It takes consistent training to keep your sales moving upward. Most people see a dramatic increase in their sales immediately following training, but it seldom lasts. Without consistent training the impulse to return to old ways of doing things is just too strong for most people to resist. Typically, sales will begin to flatten out and, in some cases, even drop to pretraining levels within a few months. Having been involved in sales training for years, I've seen this problem firsthand.

Imagine a professional football player who doesn't train or practice. He just shows up on Sunday and hopes for the best. I dare say he won't last long. Yet this is the way most sales professionals act. And then they wonder why their sales are going south. Less than 5 percent of salespeople have ever read a book on sales, let alone had any formal sales training.

Business is a game with real money involved, and you better be playing it to win. You either play the game or the game plays you. It's your choice. There is no reward for second place.

As with any profession, sales requires continuous training if you want to stay in the game.

This book doesn't contain everything there is to know about selling, and it won't make you a sales superstar. Business is too diverse, and there are simply too many products to cover in one book. If you want to become a good salesperson, you'll need lots and lots of practice.

The very best practice you can do to help boost your sales won't cost you a penny and it takes only a few minutes a day.

Here it is: Make it a point to start a conversation with three strangers in a nonsales environment every day. It sounds simple, but most people find it difficult. As children, most of us were taught to avoid strangers. In the beginning, some of these people will look at you as if you're crazy. Some will give you dirty looks. But if you do this for a month, you'll see a dramatic improvement in your sales. I promise. In no time at all, you'll be better at approaching people and gaining their trust.

I've been practicing this for years.

I'm single and I do most my "stranger talking" at grocery stores and gas stations. I might ask, "What's for dinner?" or "I sure like those shoes. Where did you find them?" or even "How about this weather?" Experience has taught me that most people have more of a problem with starting a conversation than they do with selling. I can't think of a better activity to boost sales than talking to strangers. Business isn't about products and pricing. It's about people. Learn how to engage them in conversations.

Don't try to be all things to all people. You'll need laser-like focus if you want to succeed in today's market. Early in my sales career I refused to say "no" to any request. I was hungry and needed sales badly. It didn't work. If you try to fulfill every request, you'll lose in the long run. Learn to say "no" to things that are outside of your field of expertise.

People aren't looking for a jack-of-all-trades. They're looking for specialists. The more you specialize, the more customers will come looking for you and not the other way around.

Focus comes from action, not thinking. Set your sights on the clients you want to be in business with, and take the necessary actions to gain their trust. Thinking about every detail only slows you down. You don't have time to waste. So start acting *today*.

As humans, we focus more on failure than on success. We tend to remember the things we should forget and forget the things we should remember. We view mistakes as serious failures even as we shrug off our successes as everyday occurrences. While bad days require our evaluation to correct mistakes we may have made, a good day requires even more attention. Make sure you gain the full benefit of successes by knowing what you did right. Learning how to consistently impress good habits and techniques into the intuitive mind is of real importance. Make sure you break the good day down in detail. Focus on each moment and action that brought you closer to the desired result. Make sure to embed the proper moves and actions into your mind.

One thing that can increase your sales numbers immediately is following up with existing customers. Research has shown that post-purchase follow-up actions can greatly affect customers' perceptions of our service and products. Follow up with every customer. Ask him or her if your products met expectations and if there is anything else you can do. You'll be amazed at the results.

Eighty-five percent of your success in life will be determined by the relationships you build. People are more important than products. Asking for a sale before building a relationship is like asking a stranger to marry you. Chances are that person will say, "No, thank you" and run like hell.

Change is inevitable. Most businesses use change as a mantra, but it's a hollow word. They do little more than pray that the world will change so they won't have to. Those who avoid change do so at their own peril.

If you always do what you've always done, you'll always get what you've always gotten.

Every success story in this book was due to relationships built. Every successful business I know of can credit its success to relationships. Likewise, every business failure can be traced back to poor relationships. Your friends will either make you or break you.

I've seen a lot of small business owners brought down by their friends. The scenario is basically the same. In the beginning these friends are happy to buy from you and help your business grow. Somehow they get the feeling that their single purchase is responsible for your success and they ask for discount pricing or avoid paying their bill altogether. Why is it that friends are the last to be paid? The next thing you know, you're upside-down in debt and lack the necessary cash flow to survive.

It's hard for some people to realize that their friends aren't their friends. Real friends don't ask you to carry them on your back. They pay their bills on time and don't ask for discounts. Business is about relationships, but it must go both ways.

"You want to know who your friends are? Start your own business and ask for their support."—Steve Jobs

A lot of people view big corporations as indifferent bureaucracies. In truth, corporations are people and people are corporations. Whenever you meet a new prospect, talk to that person as a friend. It'll get you a lot further than trying to impress him or her with how smart you are.

I'm frequently asked about the importance of marketing in sales. Marketing is important because you want be the first person thought of when someone needs a product or service you can provide. The problem is that a lot of people mistake marketing for sales. Marketing can produce sales, but there are limitations. Marketing has had its best success in selling low-cost items with generic appeal. Hula Hoops, Frisbees, and lawn darts come to mind. Inexpensive kitchen appliances such as Ron Popeil's famous Ronco products are another.

Business sure isn't what it used to be. Every year we get further away from "real" selling and more dependent on technology to do our selling for us. The overriding belief was mass marketing could sell anything. Today's customers demand that their individual needs be recognized and met.

Is marketing essential for success? I have never seen an ad for Mark Zuckerberg's Facebook. Have you? Facebook spread by word of mouth, and did it ever spread.

Today, marketing is best used as a tool to fill our pipelines with prospects to talk with. A good marketing plan can give you unlimited numbers of contacts. The most beautiful thing about marketing is the people who respond to your ad are prequalified. They're looking to buy, and the selling is much easier. It can be like shooting fish in a barrel.

Marketing is a good thing, but generally it's suicide to base a business on marketing alone. For that reason, I would strongly recommend you speak with a marketing expert before you embark on an expensive campaign.

Most people read sales books in hope of finding a shortcut to success. They hope that they can just learn some magical phrase or technique that will stimulate people to buy. Then they'll be set.

This book contains none of those shortcuts. If you want to learn about escalation, the take away, the bait-n-switch, price breakdown, or scarcity there are plenty of books out there with that type of information. In today's complex sales environment, however, fast talk and gimmicks are obsolete: customers are just too savvy. We're better off sticking to what works.

It would be nice if we could come up with a surefire system for success, but none exists. When it comes to sales, we're better off following principles than we are following a set system.

A system says, "Do this, then that, and the other thing and you are guaranteed a certain result." A principle says, "Try this; it works and has worked throughout recorded time." The difference between the two is crucial. Any notion that a foolproof system with guaranteed results exists is nonsense. The fact is, we find an astonishing variety of successful businesses in every niche, but no prototype.

It's not that systems are completely useless. Systems are necessary in the mass production of ordinary products in competitive markets. However, a system is of little use in the sales arena. This is because each sale is a unique moment. Each client is unique and has a unique set of problems. There just isn't a one-size-fits-all program in sales.

No one can teach you which products and services will sell and which won't, because no one knows. However, we can teach you how to present, promote, and sell your products with the highest probability of success.

The four principles of friendship, interest, simplicity, and honesty are the cornerstones on which a great sales career can be built.

Everyone wants to be great, but few are willing to commit to the grueling work that becoming great requires. Most people give up after a couple of failures. They settle for being average instead of working and striving to be the best.

Look around at successful business people. You'll find that they work hard and are enthusiastic about getting things done. They inspire and empower the people around them. They are engaged in all aspects of their life.

Attaining and retaining the best clients is a process. Getting it right is crucial. You'll get better at it with experience. No one ever got worse at selling by selling.

The End